Palgrave Studies in Economic History

Series Editor
Kent Deng
London School of Economics
London, UK

Palgrave Studies in Economic History is designed to illuminate and enrich our understanding of economies and economic phenomena of the past. The series covers a vast range of topics including financial history, labour history, development economics, commercialisation, urbanisation, industrialisation, modernisation, globalisation, and changes in world economic orders.

More information about this series at
http://www.palgrave.com/gp/series/14632

Eric L. Jones

Barriers to Growth

English Economic Development from the Norman Conquest to Industrialisation

palgrave
macmillan

Eric L. Jones
University of Buckingham
Buckingham, UK

ISSN 2662-6497 ISSN 2662-6500 (electronic)
Palgrave Studies in Economic History
ISBN 978-3-030-44273-6 ISBN 978-3-030-44274-3 (eBook)
https://doi.org/10.1007/978-3-030-44274-3

Cover illustration: Lyndon Griffith/Alamy Stock Photo

This Palgrave Macmillan imprint is published by the registered company Springer Nature Switzerland AG
The registered company address is: Gewerbestrasse 11, 6330 Cham, Switzerland

For Joel Mokyr

Acknowledgements

I am grateful to several people for help, my wife Sylvia and son Christopher for sub-editing, John Anderson and Shaun Keneally for critical readings, John Morgan for commenting on chapter 12 (Floods), and Syd Flatman for accompanying me on numerous site inspections of towns and villages.

While this book was with the publisher, Joel Mokyr sent me his review article, 'The Past and Future of Innovation: Some Lessons from Economic History', *Explorations in Economic History* 69 (2018), pp. 13–26. This is the only other direct treatment of barriers to growth that I have seen. It was therefore doubly appropriate that I had dedicated the book to him.

Praise for *Barriers to Growth*

"Jones's thesis is that the cumulative growth of national wealth over six centuries after the Norman conquest cannot alone be explained by innovations in production. Overcoming obstacles and dealing with shocks was as important in shaping economic development. *Barriers to Growth* asks us to look again at the historical record, to focus on themes which have received little attention or only specialised interest. A revised framework for interpretation emerges when the themes are woven into standard historical explanations."

—Patrick Dillon, *Emeritus Professor, College of Social Sciences and International Studies, University of Exeter*

"This book sees modern economic growth as a removal of institutional and environment barriers that held it back before the Industrial Revolution and which were gradually and unevenly relaxed at some point in the Age of Enlightenment and after. The barriers to growth before the Industrial Revolution were inertia and resistance; above all these had to be overcome. This is a work not just of erudition but of wisdom."

—Joel Mokyr, *Robert H. Strotz Professor of Arts and Sciences and Professor of Economics and History, Northwestern University*

"… a highly original and thought-provoking perspective on a major topic of debate for economic history. It challenges the existing debate by broadening its focus, drawing into the heart of the argument a welter of subtle changes that slowly transformed how markets and the flow of capital altered during the two or three centuries before the so-called take-off of the English economy."

—Robert Dodgshon, *Emeritus Professor, Department of Geography and Earth Sciences, Aberystwyth University*

Contents

PART I

The Erosion of Obstacles

CHAPTER 1

Barriers and Push Forces

Long ago I raised the question of whether economic growth may be explained in part by the stripping away of impediments.[1] I had in mind, 'the removal of tolls, internal tariffs, gilds, debasements, forced loans, confiscations, monopolies, settlement laws, sumptuary legislation and the other paraphernalia of absolutist monarchs and would-be absolutists like the Stuarts'. Conventional approaches are quite different; almost all claim to have found the prime mover. Shifting attention to negative gains from the removal of blockages implies a bolder claim. It is that an impulse to get rich was latent all along and was sufficiently widespread (which is not to say universal in time and space) to have had a big effect when unleashed. In an earlier book I considered the implications on the global stage but wish to examine it more closely here by exploring the slow dissolution of barriers in English history.[2]

My suggestion has rarely been followed but a large literature may be brought to bear on the topic. The sources drawn on here are sometimes long-standing, widely different in date and not always familiar; this should not matter if they are pertinent and have not been surpassed by more modern publications. The econometric tests now commonly applied in economic history have their merits, give or take objections to unreliable data sets and the furore in the social sciences about the meaning of statistical significance, but I prefer to cite representative examples from actual historical sources.[3] Local evidence sometimes alters one's mind about relative significance and I do not always discern the world of my ancestors in the abstractions of my profession.

E. L. Jones, *Barriers to Growth*, Palgrave Studies in Economic History,
https://doi.org/10.1007/978-3-030-44274-3_1

The following discussion moves from early and broad developments in the economy to later more specific ones. They include the reduction of materially unproductive expenditures on religious structures; unlocking land resources by means of the Dissolution of the Monasteries; ending the medieval cycle of destructive civil wars; struggling to abolish maladministration in its many forms (censorship, protectionism, corruption and so forth); lifting a vexatious levy on agriculture by means of the Tithe Commutation Act; and observing the decay of institutions which had allocated resources in a productively inefficient fashion. To these are added discussions of the economic shocks from epidemics, epizootics, weather shocks, flood, fire and so forth, and the curbing of related losses by better disaster management. Not all reported shocks or disasters prove to have been nationally important, although they were likely to have been at their most damaging in early periods. Nor could every type of shock be satisfactorily parried, at least in the period before industrialisation, but problems that threatened to reduce output seem worth investigating to assess how damaging they may have been.

This book contains a larger component of 'real world' processes than is usually found in economic history. Partly it reflects topics on which I have worked throughout my career; many have attracted interest only in specialist quarters but deserve more attention. The emphasis on agriculture will not surprise because it has always been a fairly substantial subfield within economic history. Landscape history, environmental history and disaster studies, on which I began to write early, have at long last become expanding fields. This is a healthy development even if modern practitioners move the baseline forward by scouting earlier contributions. A greater problem comes from the narrowness of conventional historians and even economic historians, who—as the new specialists are starting to lament—have seldom absorbed these topics.[4] To quote an outsider to the world of scholarship, 'it has never occurred to me that the problem—or at least the limitation—of history is that it is written by historians, scholars with a predisposition towards a particular kind of narrative. So along comes someone who knows a lot about geology and geography, and history looks completely different'.[5]

England had an intermittent but benign history of lifting burdens and reducing the impact of shocks to the economy. This was not dramatic or abrupt yet was quietly formative in releasing capital, land and labour for productive ends. When industrialisation did come about, through innovations like canalised rivers, canals and railways and the use of coal in manufacturing, this benefited from emerging in an already flexible economy—one less troubled by waste than before, as well as possessing richer and more open markets. Without this, the eventual birth of industrialisation would have been far more troubled.

Modes of economic coordination fall into the standard categories of custom, command and market. Over time the proportions changed in the direction of market allocation, which is the history of growth in a nutshell. Allocating resources and effort along customary lines had meant suppressing inequality of income at the cost of restricting individual endeavour. Historically, the market gradually, unevenly and incompletely replaced custom and may therefore be credited with opening the way for industrial growth. Command systems likewise had held back growth, since in them activity was dominated by the ruler or landowner. These men had secured their positions because their ancestors had fought for them, which meant that command systems were operated by people who did not necessarily possess commercial or managerial expertise. They had an incentive to obtain a large slice of output for themselves as rent-seekers and were not inspired to innovate in the technological sphere.

If we focus on medieval and early modern landowners in England, we find them well able to accumulate wealth. The wool trade was profitable and through it they became ever more involved with the market although using their non-market powers of command to smooth the path. They began to see the little arable holdings of the peasantry as barriers to maximising their own wealth and expelled villagers in order to turn their holdings into sheep pasture. The market thus intruded in more than an abstract sense and the process was fossilised in the ridge-and-furrow visible to this day beneath so much Midlands grass. The lantern towers of the wool churches soared up in the pastoral regions and the great rebuilding of Midlands manor houses began. The theme will recur of how many historical processes are embodied in the landscape. It is supposed that dispossessed ploughmen swelled the ranks of masterless wanderers—hence the well-known saying 'hark, hark the dogs do bark, the beggars are coming to town'.

An intriguing take on these formative processes was expressed in 1779 by Gloucestershire's topographer, Samuel Rudder.[6] In former times, Rudder proclaimed, two things operated very powerfully to hinder agriculture, meaning cultivation: the great barons preferred grazing because it released labourers to become fighting men while before the reign of Elizabeth exporting raw wool to Flanders promised huge benefits.

Agriculture was neglected, causing frequent famines and great pestilence. It is not necessary to accept Rudder's stylised model or attribution of motive to see that he was making a serious effort to explain how arable farming had been held back. There was no special return to ploughing in the Midlands triangle after the mid-sixteenth century, when rising prices might seem to have prompted it; arable expanded instead in fresh parts of the country. 'Men could decide what was the optimum use', said Maurice Beresford, 'with a freedom which they had never previously had...' when land-hunger, tradition and fear of bad harvests had bound them to growing cereals.[7] This involved exposing traditional allocations of land to market decisions.

Barriers raised the costs of investment and innovation, and when they were vanquished costs fell. Command systems could sweep some away but were better at redistributing wealth towards the powerful than at creating it. The pie was sliced rather than a larger one being baked, although the inadvertent effect was to accustom society to greater competitiveness. Over the post-medieval centuries, as we shall see, a long list of depressants was eroded or extirpated, increasingly by feedback from the forces of growth itself. The resources released might be used up in current consumption or eaten by larger and longer-lived populations, but when they did not have to be spent on repairing an endless cycle of damage they were in principle free for productive activities. So much 'unblocking' took place over the late pre-modern centuries and so many sources of loss were eliminated to make England an easier and easier venue for investment. Each episode may have been a struggle but each as an unintended consequence advanced development a little; the effects were as fruitful as many a technical breakthrough.

Only in the development economics taught in the 1950s were explicit treatments of disabilities to be found. At that period university courses quite often started with the eighteenth century, the English industrial revolution being treated as an abrupt break of trend even before Walt Rostow put the indelible label of 'take-off' on the process. Courses then jumped to the so-called Third World but when it dawned that England was not a good model for those regions the approach was abandoned. Why was England not a good model? Already too wealthy by the eighteenth century, too long supplied with functioning institutions, and uniquely supplied with inventions? Poverty in medieval or early modern times might have seemed a better analogy with contemporary less-developed countries but economics students were thought to have no appetite for syllabuses that included periods so remote. Next, any suggestion that the seventeenth-century Civil War might be an appropriate starting point faced the charge of being a covert Marxist endorsement of revolution. During the Cold War that accusation was tantamount to stifling enquiry. Instead, the industrial revolution was taken as its own starting point and presented as more or less arriving out of thin air. Cursory pronouncements about origins aside, it was virgin birth. Scholarly effort became mesmerised by any eighteenth-century innovation which might be thought (once all else was held constant) to have propelled growth.

Yet any economy suffers from multiple distortions and needs freeing from them. All resources are never fully employed or allocated to their optimal uses and old techniques are never instantly replaced by superior ones. Impediments are continually recreated; protectionism and rent-seeking are perennial. The fact that obstacles were so various and sources of physical harm so diverse has worked against thinking about the cumulative advantage of dismantling them.

Complications may seem to arise from the current opinion that world economic growth did not arrive first in England or Europe and cannot be attributed to their intrinsic features. Some other societies achieved growth earlier, China being the prime example. To what extent this really raised per capita income in China as opposed to expanding the economy there is controversial but is in any case beside the point. The large, sprawling anti-Western literature proclaims that Europe, and therefore England, was not 'first', China was. At the same time, it insists that economic growth had deplorable effects on income distribution and (in now-fashionable formulations) on the climate. Arguing about the winner of a supposed race where the finishing line is described as toxic is surely paradoxical.

Ideas did diffuse slowly around Eurasia but, a few specific imports apart, it is not clear that Western advance really depended on acquiring non-Western technology, as opposed to tackling common problems independently. Borrowings and stimulus diffusion may have occurred but so may independent evolution. Furthermore, societies such as Song China lapsed so early from their great achievements that this cannot be blamed on Western intrusions. Animus against the West seems to have roots outside scholarship and involves labelling studies of Western economic history 'Eurocentric' as if this must automatically be unacceptable. As Joel Mokyr said, the opposite of Eurocentric is eccentric, and we can reasonably continue by considering the English case.[8]

One feature of the early modern period was the taming of overtly non-market power. Settling disputes among powerful men had been likely to involve violent clashes when one lord and his entourage set out against another. This faded away, just as erecting readily defended dwellings gave way to 'wide window' mansions meant for display. From the reign of Elizabeth, it had been usual for the sons of landowners to be schooled at the Inns of Court, learning to protect their property by shuffling papers, which is to say via the law. Even the Civil War barely re-established interpersonal conflict by force of arms, the mass of the population (although not landowners or their gamekeepers) having their guns confiscated after the Restoration. The disruption, uncertainty and loss brought about by disputes and brawling in the streets can be portrayed as hampering growth; struggles in the courts were expensive too but seldom quite as directly damaging.

An alternative way of framing this is to think that resorting to violence as the means of settling disputes faded when the mutual benefits of exchange were recognised. The pace of the recognition was admittedly glacial. Christian crosses in the centre of villages and market towns had been intended to remind—nudge—medieval men into peacefulness and not to draw their daggers at any presumed slight or suspicion of cheating. The incidence of murder has been shown to have subsided gradually from the Middle Ages. The rich and powerful learned to resolve their differences other than by riding out at the head of their armed retainers, something which was coming to an end before the Civil War. Economic development increased the rewards from using non-destructive solutions to disputes; fighting might destroy possessions. Something deep was taking place when men of influence and wealth accustomed themselves to market solutions and when the judges could come out against non-market regulations like those of the guilds. It was a self-reinforcing evolution to which it is hard to assign a precise date.

Candidates for the push forces which are the favoured explanations of growth know few bounds, running as far as the 'beautiful hypothesis' that an autonomous increase in the population of earthworms improved soil fertility—shades of Charles Darwin—and raised agricultural productivity, permitting resources to flow from farming to industry. A beautiful hypothesis is one which is conceivable but for which no independent evidence exists. Prolonged changes such as the exit from feudalism or the emergence of the Protestant ethic also tend to be cited as push forces. They did leave a spoor in the sources, although without evidence that they were causes rather than correlates of growth. Intermediate candidates include a fall in interest rates, for which records do exist. Under the Stuarts rates had been high but thereafter they fell, dropping from 8–10 per cent before 1688 to three per cent by 1750.[9] Gregory King, the social statistician of the seventeenth century, thought that capital was accumulating faster than population was rising, while to the economic historian, Carlo Cipolla, the fall in interest rates was 'the true economic revolution' because it made investing cheaper.[10] The sources of these increases in productivity are easier to describe than pin down, being reputedly brought about by almost unfathomable developments such as the 'Scientific Revolution'.

Fresh obstacles to growth can always be created or at any rate feared. History was two steps forwards and one back. Two thinkers different in nationality and far apart in time, John Wesley and Joseph Schumpeter, worried that Methodism and capitalism respectively would grind to a halt because success would bring prosperity and reduce incentives to work hard and save. They did not trust the perennial power of acquisitiveness and ambition to offset the blandishments of success. From the production side, if leading entrepreneurs and industrialists did succumb to lives of ease, which they can be shown to have done when they moved their money into buying landed estates, this did remove capital from the most productive uses. It would have mattered more had there been barriers to new entrants to manufacturing industry but this was not a great problem—the rewards of one generation inspired effort in the next.

From the consumption side, Wesley and Schumpeter did not imagine the ceaseless outpouring of new goods and services that persuaded the population into working to acquire them, nor the spread of temptations down the income scale. A more recent authority, Mancur Olson, was known for urging the rise of distributional coalitions of self-regarding interests which curb the mobility of factors of production, the rate of innovation and the reallocation of resources. His widely cited view does not perhaps allow sufficiently for contrary tendencies in competitive markets but is consistent with the injustice when assets were acquired unfairly and the unequal distribution of wealth was perpetuated.[11] The resultant ossification affected the land sector but, although manufacturing suffered indirect disabilities with which this book will deal, it was not on the whole afflicted in the ways that Wesley, Schumpeter and Olson feared.

Against the impression that checks on growth can be all-powerful, William Marshall would have found the expansion of the market congenial to his view that customary items continually and subtly alter, hard though it is to observe this behind old fixed labels. His position, that stagnation is silently overcome by incremental advances, sits well with most history of the dissolution of barriers. In England, the presence or rise of countervailing checks revealed itself by the mutability of economic regions, with new ones developing even as others became, so to speak, mired in old technologies and trades. Distributions may have seemed unchanging while welling up scarcely noticed elsewhere. Generalisations about the economic significance of locational shifts are scarce despite innumerable studies of individual firms, industries, towns and regions in one historical period or another.

England is geophysically stable, London for example being reported to have suffered only a single death by earthquake, and that in 1580. Other shocks to the economy nevertheless remained plentiful but by the seventeenth century, at least, capital was available to repair damage, most strikingly after the Great Fire of London in 1666. The jurist, Mathew Hale, devised the Fire Court which overrode private property rights in the interests of reconstruction, just as guild restrictions on the entry of builders from the provinces were set aside. Wars, the Fire and the Plague were not severe enough to set the economy back because of this dismantling of institutional barriers and because enough capital had already been accumulated to cope. The incentive to reinvest was strong because abnormal gains might be expected during catch-up. Writing in 1776, Adam Smith was the leading exponent of the economy's resilience and ability to continue growing despite a litany of shocks. No conflagration recurred on the scale of the Great Fire. (When an event is called 'Great' this usually means it was the last big one in its category or locality.) Nor did the plague, famine or other major shocks return on a national scale.

Adam Smith and after him Macaulay discerned the cumulative growth of national wealth over six centuries and unlike some of their successors were interested in the way its path had been eased. To repeat, the conventional novelties of the industrial revolution cannot account for such a prolonged trend. Here we reverse the question and ask not what pushed growth forwards but what had already challenged the obstacles. Adam Smith understood the power of England's pre-industrial economy when he referred in 1776 to 'the happiest and most fortunate period of them all, that which has passed since the restoration'.[12] National ruin might have been anticipated from a string of calamities: 'the fire and the plague of London, the two Dutch wars, the disorder of the revolution, the war in Ireland, the four expensive French wars… together with the two rebellions of 1715 and 1745'. Yet ruin did not happen.

Writing in 1848 Macaulay generalised the phenomenon into a story of continuous, or at any rate continual, growth despite the numerous shocks. He contended that wealth had been greater under the Tudors than under the Plantagenets, greater under the Stuarts than under the Tudors, greater at the Restoration than when the Long Parliament sat, and 'in spite of maladministration, of extravagance, of public bankruptcy, of two costly and unsuccessful wars, of the pestilence and of the fire, it was greater on the day of the death of Charles II than on the day of his Restoration'.[13] Macaulay did not have national income figures to substantiate his tale but he did base his narrative on a supremely detailed grasp of English history, whose peculiarities elude students determined to cut the Gordian Knot. We may therefore now look at the negative gains from the evaporation of major obstacles and from the softening of physical blows.

Notes

1. E. L. Jones, 'Institutional Determinism and the Rise of the Western World', *Economic Inquiry* XII (1) (1974), p. 123.
2. E. L. Jones, *Growth Recurring: Economic Change in World History* (Oxford: Oxford University Press, 1988).
3. John Hatcher and Judy Z. Stephenson (eds.), *Seven Centuries of Unreal Wages* (Basingstoke: Palgrave Macmillan, 2018).
4. On the neglect of the physical environment and non-agrarian resources, see S. Rippon, '"Making the Most of a Bad Situation?" Glastonbury Abbey and the Exploitation of Wetland Resources in the Somerset Levels', *Medieval Archaeology* 48 (2004), p. 94 n. clxi, and on the failure of historians to interact with disaster studies, Daniel R. Curtis et al., 'History and the Social Sciences: Shock Therapy with Medieval Economic History as the Patient', *Social Science History* 40 (4) (2016), pp. 751–774.
5. Malcolm Gladwell, interviewed in *Review*, 86 (7 Sept 2019), p. 5.
6. Samuel Rudder, *A New History of Gloucestershire* (Nonsuch 2006 [1779]), p. 22.
7. Maurice Beresford, *The Lost Villages of England* (Gloucester: Alan Sutton, 1983 [1954]), pp. 213–214.
8. Eric L. Jones, 'England as the Source of the Great Divergence', *Tijdschrift voor Sociale en Economische Geschiedenis* 12 (2) (2015), pp. 79–92.
9. L. S. Pressnell (ed.), *Studies in the Industrial Revolution* (London: The Athlone Press, 1960), pp. 211–212.

10. E. L. Jones, *The European Miracle* (Cambridge: Cambridge University Press, 1981), p. 41.
11. David Miles, 'The Half Life of Economic Injustice', Paper to conference, 'Accounting for the Wealth of Nations' April 2019, on the website of the Centre for Economic Policy Research, especially p. 6 and n. 3 on land acquisition in England.
12. Adam Smith, *An Inquiry into the Nature and Causes of the Wealth of Nations* (New York: The Modern Library, 1937 [1776]), p. 328.
13. Quoted by John U. Nef, *War and Human Progress* (New York: W. W. Norton, 1968), p. 275.

CHAPTER 2

Military and Ecclesiastical Building

We start with the broadest and earliest matter, the burden imposed by tying up capital in structures designed to intimidate. Quickly after the Conquest in 1066, William I began a programme of castle building so extensive that by 1085 about 100 defensive fortifications had been erected. Funding came from squeezing resources out of the conquered Saxon population, including compulsory labour, although this may not have been quite as damaging as it seems because much of the work might have been done outside the crop-growing season. Nevertheless the net effect was unlikely to have raised living standards.

The first wave of castles was of the motte-and-bailey type, surmounted by wooden palisades. The obvious disadvantage of building in wood ensured that it was replaced by stone during the next hundred years or so. A trend also began towards making castles more comfortable residences. The subsequent history of castle building fluctuated according to military need (it was upwards during the Anarchy of the early twelfth century and when Edward I set about overawing the Welsh with some very grand castles) and later with the shifting balance of attack and defence in weaponry. After 1450 building new military structures virtually ceased, apart from coastal defences and a brief resurgence of fortification during the seventeenth-century Civil War, which was followed by the slighting of many defensive works.

The heaviest burden of construction came in the poorest early periods. Whereas castles were of some use to the economy through keeping the peace, this had to be paid for. They were solid and strong enough to last

E. L. Jones, *Barriers to Growth*, Palgrave Studies in Economic History,
https://doi.org/10.1007/978-3-030-44274-3_2

for almost six centuries after the conquest, which meant that they had a long life during which they continued to need maintenance and remained an imposition on productive sectors of the economy. It is noteworthy that this particular form of unproductive expenditure faded right away in the century before industrialisation. Warfare had by then become more mobile and the potential need for fixed defensive positions had evaporated. Monarchs still needed somewhere to live and display their pre-eminence, however, which involved heavy expenditure on palaces meant more for display than defence. In terms of excessive expenditure, royal residences therefore replaced in some measure the imposition that castle building had begun. Henry VIII built himself sumptuous palaces. Elizabeth I built none, preferring to progress around the houses of her more aspiring subjects, but extravagant construction returned with James I early in the seventeenth century. Large outlays recurred in certain later reigns; the cost of building work at Buckingham Palace exceeded estimates and had reached £500,000 by 1829. The number of former royal residences is high and many continue in use today, although it would be hard to argue that the total burden is as onerous as in earlier centuries.

Another potential burden had arisen early through the building of ecclesiastical structures. On the face of it, they were not intended to promote mundane growth and although parish churches had some secular uses the initial expenditure diverted resources that from the material point of view might have been spent more productively. Most churches were already in existence by the end of the twelfth century, following a post-Conquest boom of construction which included erecting enormously costly cathedrals that took years to complete. One estimate is that by 1200 there were 8500–9000 churches in England, the vast majority served by stone churches many of which were then in the process of being expanded. Building parish churches took place in waves, which renders hazardous generalising about a long-term downturn in activity.[1] Three problems appear. First comes uncertainty about the timing of construction, let alone its cost; the focus of most studies of churches is the astonishingly intricate history of architectural or art appreciation which is ordinarily blind to economic aspects.[2] Beyond the reasonable surmise that the Conqueror's knights, rich with plunder, were the ones who funded the twelfth-century boom, questions about how much was paid and who paid it are seldom raised. Secondly, it is uncertain how much money was thereafter consumed in maintaining and elaborating the buildings. Thirdly is the intractable, virtually philosophical, difficulty of deciding how far ecclesiastical edifices contributed to material well-being. The very act of building—spread over decades, even centuries in the case of cathedrals—was not ethereal; it spurred quarrying and gave work to skilled and unskilled labour. How far the completed results contributed to everyday life is moot but contribute they plainly did.

That churches squandered resources which could have been better used in very poor societies is readily acceptable to many social scientists but mere opinion does not guarantee its truth. The innumerable cathedrals, churches and monasteries to be found across medieval England fulfilled more secular functions than might be imagined.[3] What other nationally distributed institutions were there to shelter communal gatherings, act as town halls or foreshadow the welfare state? Pastoral care radiated from the premises, which were used as marketplaces as well as meeting places. Initials and other scratches on window sills are held to show the functioning of churches as schools. Nor could the medieval church be accused of unworldliness in that absolutely every type of fund-raising device was employed to support building efforts, many involving the parading of fake relics and as it were acting like a voluntary tax. Although the basic architectural stock has usually survived, recurrent expenditure was needed to extend or maintain it; parish churches have been endlessly altered, even bodged up. Add to this the lack of numerical data and the topic seems unmanageable. Computations of all the activity viewed as a return on investment would be arbitrary, not to mention foolhardy.

Constructing an index for the inter-period comparison of building costs, either ecclesiastical or secular (such as the transition from castles to palaces and country mansions), would be fatally challenged by the data vacuum, the changing value of money, and the lack of baselines such as secure knowledge of GDP in early periods. Two generations ago, H. T. Johnson did make a brave attempt to quantify the cost of cathedral building but his exercise, unfamiliar and uncomfortable as it was to many students of religion, was not surprisingly thought unpersuasive.[4] As was observed by C. R. Cheney, who was far from averse to considering economic consequences and was well informed on the subject, the surviving records are just not good enough to calculate the scale of receipts secured by the extraordinary medieval campaigns to fund ecclesiastical building.[5] An additional likelihood is that parish churches were built as showpieces by many a local lord; if so, there was an opportunity cost to what would have been almost vanity projects.

Resources had been lavished in medieval times on improving the churches with successively larger windows and ornamenting them with wall paintings and painted glass, among other features. Despite the difficulties of computation, the arrival of Protestantism with its less magical rituals and the Puritan destruction of church effigies reduced the elaboration, give or take what John Goodall calls an 'extraordinary' phase of rebuilding and refurnishing after 1620.[6] The shift from Roman Catholicism to a determinedly Protestant England was accompanied by more austerity in the buildings as part of a long slide down the hierarchy of ostentation from painted chancels towards the various plain styles of Nonconformist chapels and the even plainer meeting houses of the Society of Friends (Quakers). Money was admittedly spent in the churches on buying and sometimes ornamenting dedicated family pews, while in the seventeenth and eighteenth centuries certain families spent large sums, relative to their personal wealth, on monuments and effigies, but at the national level this was scarcely significant.

Economic growth would have made display more, not less, affordable but the monuments in parish churches became progressively less ornate as they moved from the ostentation of Tudor effigies to the still boastful but far cheaper wall brasses of Victorian times. The Nonconformists had long met in rooms in private houses, often kitchens, but following the Wesleyan surge of the late eighteenth century they began to erect chapels. The buildings differed in style according to sects and did not closely mimic parish churches. It was the tombs outside that soon competed with those in Anglican churchyards, demonstrating an element of status-seeking in Nonconformist worship. But only a tiny fraction of chapel-goers marked their earthly success in this way or could afford to do so.

Whether the housing of the clergy falls into the category of excessive expenditure depends on one's attitude to Anglicanism. By the 'age of ecclesiastical dilapidation' during the eighteenth century the incumbents of many parishes were housed in near-mansions yet elsewhere the rectory house was tumbledown. Some of the clergy were too rich, partly through pluralism, which meant they were often absent from one or more of the livings they held and were little concerned with the accommodation offered. Others were too poor, which likewise meant scant attention to their domestic shelter. Efforts at amending this situation awaited the first half of the nineteenth century, when 600 new churches were built and £1.5 million of taxpayers' money was transferred to the Church Building Commissioners.[7] This may seem a large sum but as a proportion of national wealth ecclesiastical expenditure, although fluctuating, continued to tend downwards over the centuries.

Very few new churches had been put up between 1540 and the Restoration of 1660, which then produced a bout of repair and new furnishing to deal with the damage and neglect of the Civil War and Interregnum, a bout further inspired in London by the need to fill the vacuum created by the Great Fire of 1666. The fire destroyed 86 churches and state funds were added to private money to rebuild them, making this, according to Goodall, 'a state endeavour'. A study of Germany which treats construction as a means of summarising the allocation of resources finds that religious construction had declined during the Reformation, especially in Protestant regions, whereas secular construction increased, especially on administrative offices that presumably had direct utility.[8]

In England the stock of churches seldom needed much further supplementation before the late eighteenth and nineteenth centuries and the surge in new churches funded by government grants in 1818 and 1824. The established church was then belatedly seeking to counter Nonconformist competition and catch up with the growth of urban-industrial populations for which it had hitherto made little provision. The Victorians provided 'stupendous sums of money' to refurnish old churches and build new ones. In England, luxury houses, built by the rich, reinforced, even replaced, ecclesiastical extravagance but at the national level any major diversion of investment from materially productive ends had come much earlier, during the medieval erection of churches and cathedrals. Modern church building in no way competes with earlier periods. As Goodall concludes about churches in the twentieth century, 'it's hard to point to another period in the thousand-year history of these buildings when they have stood still for so long'.

Notes

1. W. G. Hoskins, *The Heritage of Leicestershire* (Leicester: City of Leicester, 1950), pp. 36–41. See also Colin Platt, *The Parish Churches of Medieval England* (London: Chancellor Press, 1995).
2. I have found the best guide to architectural and artistic matters to be John Goodall, *Parish Church Treasures* (London: Bloomsbury Continuum, 2015). It does make some pertinent references to occasions for expenditure.
3. For the wide distribution of monasteries see the map in R. A. Donkin, in H. C. Darby (ed.), *A New Historical Geography of England Before 1600* (Cambridge: Cambridge University Press, 1973), p. 96.

4. H. T. Johnson, 'Cathedral Building and the Medieval Economy', *Explorations in Entrepreneurial History* 4 (3) (1967), pp. 191–210.
5. C. R. Cheney, 'Church Building in the Middle Ages', *Bulletin of the John Rylands Library* xxxiv (1957), pp. 20–30; Christiane Klapisch, 'Cathedrales gothique et economie medieval', *Annales ESC* 25 (1) (1970), pp. 226–227.
6. Goodall, *Parish Church Treasures* (2015), pp. 152–154.
7. Anthea Jones, *A Thousand Years of the English Parish* (Moreton-in-Marsh: The Windrush Press, 2000), p. 158.
8. Davide Cantoni, Jeremiah E. Dittmar, and Noam Yuchtman, *Reallocation and Secularization: The Economic Consequence of the Protestant Reformation* (CEP Discussion Papers, CEPDP1485, London School of Economics, 2017).

CHAPTER 3

Dissolution of the Monasteries

The next example is more detailed, debating a thesis that the sixteenth-century Dissolution of the Monasteries overturned their conservative management of agriculture and replaced it with the enterprise of the gentry class. This argument, in the research paper by Leander Heldring et al. which is discussed here, is highly ambitious in proceeding over several centuries from this early event to industrialisation as a whole.[1] In itself, the notion that the gentry played a part in industrialisation would not surprise. They were a large class and Mingay cited estimates that during the period from 1690 to 1873 they owned about half of the area of England and Wales, with the percentage gradually increasing throughout that time.[2] They had land, other assets, the example of their neighbours, family connections with business and in each generation recruited additional individuals with commercial capital and prior business experience. Nor is it surprising that they, or some of them, were involved in improving agriculture. But they were scarcely the leaders and in Mingay's view the most enterprising landowners during the eighteenth century were the old landed families. The incremental adoption of new crops and methods by working farmers probably made even more difference.

The recent paper by Heldring et al. (hereafter Heldring) takes the contrary, thoroughly positive, view of the gentry's contribution. This bold and aggregative work makes the gentry pivotal to economic growth by claiming that increased farm productivity and the entire industrial revolution came about because their class had seized the market opportunities handed to them by the Dissolution—in short, through the removal

E. L. Jones, *Barriers to Growth*, Palgrave Studies in Economic History,
https://doi.org/10.1007/978-3-030-44274-3_3

of the archaisms and inflexibilities of monastic farming. My approach will be to put forward counters to this triumphalist and virtually monocausal case. The aim is to bias the argument as far as possible against the conclusion which I ultimately reach: that, while not bringing about the unique sweep proposed in Heldring, the Dissolution did remove obstacles to growth. The gentry who replaced the monks were nothing like as progressive as Heldring claims and a direct link between their rise, the fall of the monasteries and the much later industrialisation is rather far-fetched. Yet a case remains that the Dissolution did help to free the land market and encourage agricultural development.

Pushing the industrial revolution back to one true cause—in this case the Dissolution—through all the subsequent exigencies of history risks the rejoinder that other events might equally have been its origin, singly or in combination. Distinguishing among candidates is not simple, nor is deciding at what date a potentially infinite regress should be halted. A strong defence of the proposed inception point would be required and the implied theory of path dependence would need to be fleshed out. A determinist and monocausal thesis—kick-started by the Dissolution—follows the traditional form of explanation in that all other factors need to be lined up waiting to be set in motion. That is surely too stringent. Nevertheless, a large array of correlations is presented by the Heldring paper to support their argument. Their thesis, then, is that the Dissolution's creation of a land market, together with the entrepreneurial zeal of the gentry who benefited from it, is what caused the industrial revolution. The Dissolution is also made to explain the geographical distribution of subsequent industrial activity.

The thesis is certainly congenial to the argument that removing obstacles was formative for the ascent to growth. But might not this particular interpretation be overdrawn? Two underlying assumptions can be challenged, one relating to purportedly intrinsic market behaviour and the other concerning the supposed maximising behaviour of the gentry. First is the supposition that land released from the rigid grip of religious houses was automatically 'allocated to more productive use'. No doubt some of it was, but this is an article of faith, not a historical fact, and is countered by evidence of unproductive and even economically depressive expenditures on the part of the gentry. The claim that gentry rather than monastic ownership raised productivity overextends both their behaviour and the torpor of the monastic orders. The gentry are described as a 'commercially oriented class of farmers', using the land more efficiently via investment and innovation. Yet many of the acres acquired at the Dissolution went to men who had already been the administrators of monastic property and who used the land to round out their own estates. No evidence is advanced to show that administrators or gentry typically engaged in husbandry themselves, rather than renting out land to tenants who undertook the actual farming. According to Bettey's close study of the West Country, although most land was sold at market prices this made little difference to the tenants, who continued to be responsible for rent and tithes.[3] With respect to the entire nation, a similarly cautious note is struck by Woodward in *The Dissolution of the Monasteries*.[4] Woodward found no essential difference in estate management between the new lay landowners and the previous monks and nuns; he detected no new class of landowners emerging as a result of the Dissolution.

The mechanism at the heart of the Heldring case is the opposite of this, urging that the Dissolution created a land market, modernising agrarian institutions and explaining the industrial revolution, which is depicted as essentially complete by 1838. Yet at that date, many archaic institutions persisted without replacement or modification. Mingay's findings were that estates were often dominated by ancient arrangements, limiting landowner action vis a vis their tenants, and inhibiting improvement.[5] It is pertinent that Woodward notes all landowners, lay or ecclesiastical, as perpetually involved in disputes to protect titles to their lands and leases.[6] Additional broad acres were well worth acquiring but that was not the end of the matter; they had to be defended against other landowners. The inviolate and adamantine nature of landed property under the law is therefore brought into question and a slow churning of ownership is to be expected. One might conclude that the Dissolution was primarily a land-grab which, despite all changes of individual ownership, established an unequal system that has remained impervious to reform.[7]

The Heldring insistence that forms of tenure impeding productivity gains were renegotiated is at the least exaggerated; no direct evidence or chronology is supplied. Some antique tenures and institutions for allocating land continued well into, and even beyond, the nineteenth century. Courts leet, soke mills, perambulations and the beating of the bounds persisted through any period that could be labelled the industrial revolution. The Custom of the County, establishing different local restrictions on the rights of outgoing and incoming tenants, was still potent during the nineteenth century.[8] The stipulations could be insisted on unless a lease expressly excluded them; moreover common usage was sufficient to establish a right. Sir Thomas Littleton's fifteenth-century *Tenures* was still occasionally cited in the law courts during the twentieth century. At least one court leet lasted until 1977. During the early twenty-first century, local authorities occasionally draw on enclosure awards to decide modern routes and boundaries, and there are country solicitors who retain old archives lest they still prove useful.

Boundaries were sometimes ancient and followed permanent and barely contestable landscape features but others continued to be vague and caused just as frequent disputes as that endemic source of contention, tithes. In the sixteenth and early seventeenth centuries conflicts could turn violent and the electioneering of subsequent times was anything but calm. Not infrequently, the location of boundaries and rights of way depended on 'shepherd's memory', that is recollection by the oldest inhabitant. Rolling hedges were rife and were a regular, or rather irregular, device for enlarging holdings at the expense of common moorland and heath. Trees remained as boundary markers despite their relative transience. Proposals for a Land Registry that would have regularised data on property ownership were blocked by the legal profession century after century.

Even parish boundaries, which Heldring declares changed little, were far from guaranteed or there would have been no call for Rogation-tide perambulations and beatings of the bounds. Boundaries were often frozen from the thirteenth century until the spate of parish creations after 1830 but nevertheless might still be altered to go around parks.[9] In addition, as late as 1836, over 180 boundaries still needed to be formally clarified by the Tithe Commissioners. Tate's classic *The Parish Chest* states outright that 'in the days before ordnance maps, disputes often arose as to the position of parish boundaries…'. He observes that beating the bounds was 'much more than an agreeable and picturesque old custom', while Angus Winchester's book on parish boundaries contains an entire section on disputes.[10] The excellent Berkshire Record Office catalogue of 1952 lists documents showing that Berkshire and Oxfordshire justices were determining the parish boundary of Whitchurch and other riparian parishes as late as the mid-1870s. Treating parishes as wholly fixed units in the landscape is therefore unwise. Any notion of a system that was straightforwardly or speedily responsive to economic inducements might be analytically convenient but is historically speaking a chimera. If the Dissolution or the gentry radically altered agrarian England, they took their time about it.

The economically unproductive side of behaviour by the gentry should be stressed. Admittedly some among their number were energetic and innovative but that was only to be expected given their resources of land (and need for ready money), frequent origins in commerce, and the sheer fact that they included so many different individuals acting over more than one century. It was typical of many among the gentry to spend time and money on the pursuit of status and leisure. Heldring asserts on the other hand that the Dissolution encouraged people with a 'capitalistic' preference and the new owners 'likely' bought land with a profit motive in mind. Dare one suggest that using the American 'likely' reveals slightly anachronistic expectations and a misunderstanding of motives? The surmise is contrary to the conclusion by Mingay, who actually studied the gentry, that 'there is no need to invoke the bourgeois capitalistic spirit to explain why some landowners rose further or faster. The factors affecting a family's income and expenditure were many and complex, and the way in which they managed their estates was only one of these…'.[11] It is reasonable to assume that some did have profit in mind or that it was part of their aim but ambition does not guarantee an outcome. Heldring notes that the gentry sat in Parliament to enact laws to subsidise farming via export bounties or at any rate to help those sections of agriculture within reach of the east coast ports from which grain could be shipped to the continent. They certainly did legislate in that way but agriculture has various products and the paper's conception of the 'wheat suitability' of land is too narrow. As late as 1800 only two-thirds of grain consumed in the domestic market—much the biggest outlet—was wheat.[12]

Purely social motives for holding land are indicated by a profusion of testimony. Land offered access to the higher reaches of rural society and politics, as well as a variety of enticing amenities. The last point is crucial. The acquisition of an estate or enough farmland to piece an estate together was an aspect of social climbing. Land was put into ornamental parks, sometimes at demonstrable cost in foregone income. Farm practice was commonly subordinated to game rearing and to some extent fox hunting. Rivers that had been sources of fish protein for local people were increasingly privatised for elite fly-fishing, paralleling the distributional inequities of the much better known enclosure of land, which in any case was not self-evidently meant to improve agriculture as opposed to amassing more land to be rented out and farmed by existing methods. The increase of agricultural output that did take place—despite everything, one might almost say—tends to obscure the unproductive processes dragging against it.

Gross figures of ownership or output do not reveal the social element in gentry life. Admittedly landowners were prominent among the people who showed cattle and other produce at agricultural shows in the late eighteenth century and after, but this may be misleading about the seriousness of their farming. Prizes at shows were indicated by rosettes and other symbols, indicating competition for non-pecuniary rewards. Awards might later translate into commercial advantage—the sale of stud rights especially—or they might not. The standard criticism of agricultural shows is that they conduce to the 'prize marrow fallacy' whereby prestige attaches to the size of an entry rather than its profitability. It calls into question the Heldring idea of a capitalist mentality; agriculturally speaking, the gentry were as much or more interested in esteem as hard cash.

They were definitely fixated on amenity, as witness the building of country houses and extension of parks, the latter often formed by converting fields into picturesque but not very productive vistas. The desire for amenity at the cost of diverting investment from productive activities is a much underplayed motive for expenditure. Most telling was the continual privatisation of rights of way. Contrary to the assertion by economists that privatisation moves assets into the hands of those who will use them most productively, 'road capture' had no such effect—the assertion is an a priori proposition which ignores one of the gentry's commonest practices. It is little more than dogma. By diverting or obliterating roads or downgrading them into footpaths, all for the sake of privacy or aesthetics, and thereby obliging users to travel a long way round, the gentry imposed a cost on society and the economy. This was done in a very large number of cases.

During the late sixteenth or seventeenth centuries there had been a little-studied shift of elite opinion in favour of market solutions, most evident in the judicial rejection of guild restrictions. This progressive tendency continued to struggle against endemic or recurrent rent-seeking, undermining the idea of straightforwardly unidirectional history. Of particular note was the gradual improvement of transport and communications, especially the latter but including unsung improvements in the construction of the road or stage waggons in which most goods were carried.[13] Long before the industrial revolution, the linking of settlements and hence markets, encouraged competition and resulted in certain towns (to say nothing of London) growing vigorously while others grew little, stagnated or even shrank. The extent of the competition is emphasised by the way certain towns specialised in particular products. There was ferment, visible in Defoe's *Tour*, whereby some towns rose and others fell, a confused picture for which Defoe admitted he could provide no general explanation. Few modern authors have noted this feature and in books on history the vitality of the English economy before the late eighteenth century can be overshadowed by subsequent industrialisation.

Towns and whole regions could now trade on their comparative advantage, meaning that silent shifts accompanied pre-industrial urban growth. Charles Wilson mentions the 'confused patchwork' of early modern industry and Sidney Pollard refers to 'the shifting kaleidoscope of industrial specialization before 1750'.[14] The net effect was the elimination of small places in favour of larger ones producing for more than local consumption. Though they were opposites, decline and growth were both responses to the expansion of the market. It is not clear that the more active land market fostered by the Dissolution was responsible for this.

The prosperity of towns and districts was also rearranged by slowly changing agricultural distributions. One alteration was the gradual inversion of land use whereby the centre of gravity of cereal production moved from the clay vales to the light soils of the downs and wolds. This followed the introduction of fodder crops on which sheep could be fed and so manure the thin soils of the higher ground in Lowland England. It was an unintended, or initially unintended, consequence of technical changes in methods of cropping, patterned by ecology rather than by any overall change of ownership.[15] Some of the gentry presumably lost out as a result of the falling prosperity of their cereal-growing tenants in the clay vales, except to the extent that cattle husbandry and cheesemaking compensated, whereas others gained from cropping on the hills.

A fundamental alteration was the remorseless movement of industry towards the north. It predated the extensive industrial use of coal and came about for complex reasons, most evidently—as indicated—by economies of scale built on product specialisation, together with the competition among towns encouraged by improved communications. Between the sixteenth and eighteenth centuries, a sizeable number of towns disappeared from the ranks of prosperous settlements. In 1662 eight of the ten biggest provincial towns in England lay south-east of a line from the Severn to the Wash, whereas two centuries later only two of the top ten fell within the same zone. This might be attributed to the coal-based industrial revolution since, once coal was widely adopted in industry, the northward shift was incontrovertibly magnified. The coincidence encourages the belief that industrialisation was *caused* by coal, whereas coal and steam more plausibly formed the second stage of a process already under way.

Even more to the point, the process involved not merely the growth of (northern) industry but the corresponding and seldom recognised decline of myriad small industries in the south, where both population and manufacturing had initially been thickest. It meant the deskilling of former non-agricultural workers in the south. The gentry did little to succour southern manufacturing, since what they preferred was the production of handmade, bespoke craft goods made in workshops. They were not enthusiastic about independent manufacturers or workforces on their doorsteps and sometimes actively resisted on grounds of amenity. And what purchasing power they did exert locally was compromised in the late eighteenth century by their tendency to spend time and money in the new spa towns and to buy fashionable goods from London—features again facilitated by the improvement of communications.

The decline of the southern industry questions the significance of an equation between former monastic lands and the economic advance of lands held by the gentry. The equation might be defended for Yorkshire but much of the West Country and most of the south and east of England were dominated, Mingay notes, by gentry estates, and these regions were deindustrialising. The examples of gentry industrial enterprise cited by Heldring refer to the coal districts where opportunities for mining existed and where encouraging talk about prospects doubtless took place among neighbours. Evidence of gentry enterprise is certainly to be found in the numerous efforts at finding coal in the south but the point is they were failures. Despite Heldring's bid to explain not only economic growth but its geographical distribution, and despite the references to coal, his paper's proxy for industry is a narrow one: the presence of textile mills in 1838. No mention is made of the industrially declining areas that were so full of gentry and the paper's claim that existing explanations of the distribution of industry are 'simple geography' is a travesty of their complexity and faithfulness to detailed evidence.[16] Ironically, the Heldring paper itself shifts to geographical, i.e. spatial, explanations when it locates enterprise in parishes close to towns and those with the implausible proxy of high 'wheat suitability'. But spatial distributions *tout court* account for little; they need economic or historical impulses to activate them.

The eventual leap into the machine age may have been on a narrow front but industrialisation and deindustrialisation were otherwise broad processes with many influences reinforcing one another. The complex sources of growth, or perhaps one should say of a market that could readily respond to growth, included the activities of Nonconformists and Quakers. They were rarely gentry, although in Victorian times successful ones did occasionally buy estates (before very often converting to the Church of England). Of particular interest was the role of small inventors, manufacturers and entrepreneurs in the north-west, especially south-east Lancashire. These were independent men who had acquired capital in the sixteenth century when rents lagged behind prices. Some were watchmakers engaged in solving technical problems in such a way that the real prices of watches came tumbling down in the hundred years before the conventional start of the industrial revolution. Some of the makers were hired away to help solve the (probably less challenging) problems of constructing textile machinery in the Lancashire mills. Not for nothing did Richard Arkwright refer to cotton-spinning machinery as clockwork.

Economics aims to identify the factors acting beneath the bewildering surface of manifold events and to account for them in a systematic rather than ad hoc fashion. There is a difference, however, between coping with reality via a consistent analytical framework and stereotyping that reality in order to ease the task. Gross correlations between monastic dispossession and the rise of the gentry notwithstanding, there are reasons for doubting the force of any of the single factors held to account for industrial growth. There were too many contingencies and too much time had passed. 'Hampering history', as Donald Coleman called it, baffles attempts to assert monocausal explanations of the industrial revolution. And as Mingay observed, local studies 'reveal how excessively over-simple are explanations of complex changes which turn on some single key factor.'[17] Such opinions about methodology might be dismissed as only to be expected from traditional economic historians but they are the views of people deeply familiar with the sources. There is a solid case for arguing that change was idiosyncratic and hard to routinize.

The rise in agricultural productivity occurred despite all the institutional quirks and despite the capital sequestered by the gentry, not to mention the aristocracy, in rural adornments of limited productive value. The role of the gentry—the active link in the Heldring paper—was extremely mixed and included a large dash, maybe a preponderance, of rent-seeking. It is difficult to attribute industrialisation to them or specifically to the release of large areas of land by the Dissolution of the Monasteries which is supposed to have animated them. I have gone out of my way to minimise their role but nevertheless there is something in the notion that a degree of conservatism was unblocked by the Dissolution. The problems are the narrow definition of industrialisation and the speed with which agrarian change was supposed to have occurred. Yet a more fluid and competitive land market, with many more participants than the relatively small number of monastic houses, presumably did aid agricultural development. Even allowing for Bettey's point that many of the purchasers of monastic lands were the same lay people who had been managing them anyway, their sheer numbers do suggest more competition and innovation. The gentry were responsible for part of the novelty in crops, rotations and livestock breeding but the larger part came more often and more directly from their tenants. Despite the gentry's greater prominence in the secondary literature, working farmers brought about more of agriculture's advance during the post-Dissolution centuries.

Notes

1. Leander Heldring, James A. Robinson, and Sebastian Vollmer, *Monks, Gents and Industrialists: The Long-Run Impact of the Dissolution of the Monasteries* (NBER Working Paper No. 21450, August 2015). For a contrary view of the role of the gentry, see Eric L. Jones, *Locating the Industrial Revolution: Inducement and Response* (Singapore: World Scientific, 2010); E. L. Jones, 'Gentry Culture and the Stifling of Industry', *Journal of Socio-economics* 47 (2013), pp. 185–192; and Eric L. Jones, *Landed Estates and Rural Inequality in English History* (Basingstoke: Palgrave Macmillan, 2018).
2. G. E. Mingay, *The Gentry: The Rise and Fall of a Ruling Class* (London: Longman, 1976), p. 59.
3. J. H. Bettey, *The Suppression of the Monasteries in the West Country* (Gloucester: Alan Sutton, 1989), p. 133.
4. C. W. O. Woodward, *The Dissolution of the Monasteries* (London: Blandford Press, 1966), especially pp. 10–11, 131–132, 168.
5. Mingay, *The Gentry* (1986), p. 86; Peter M. Carrozzo, 'Tenures in Antiquity: A Transformation of Concurrent Ownership for Modern Relationships', *Marquette Law Review* 85 (2) (2001), especially p. 439; E. L. Jones, 'Economics Without History: Objections to the Rights Hypothesis', *Continuity and Change* 28 (3) (2013), pp. 323–346.
6. Woodward, *Dissolution* (1966), p. 9.

7. David Miles, 'The Half Life of Economic Injustice', Paper to conference, 'Accounting for the Wealth of Nations' April 2019, on the website of the Centre for Economic Policy Research.
8. William Woodfall, *Woodfall's Practical Treatise on the Law of Landlord and Tenant* (London: S. Sweet et al., 1837). As an illustration of persistent county differences, a Cornish family travelled by train from Truro to Swindon and Highworth with all its furniture, cattle and farm implements in order to rent a Gloucestershire farm from 29 September 1891. Having already had to tranship everything at Swindon because the branch line to Highworth was a different gauge, only on arrival did it find the Gloucestershire removal date was not until 11th October! (Ruth Phillips, *Short Story of a Farmer: Samuel John Phillips* [Privately printed c. 1972]).
9. Oliver Rackham, *The History of the Countryside* (London: J. M. Dent and Sons, 1987), p. 19.
10. W. E. Tate, *The Parish Chest* (Cambridge: University Press, 1969), p. 74; Angus Winchester, *Discovering Parish Boundaries* (Princes Risborough: Shire Publications, 1990).
11. Mingay, *The Gentry* (1986), p. 57.
12. E. J. T. Collins, 'Dietary Change and Cereal Consumption in Britain in the Nineteenth Century', *Agricultural History Review* 23 (2) (1975), pp. 97–115, at 114.
13. Farm waggons are readily found in rural museums but road waggons, once ubiquitous, have almost dropped out of history.
14. C. Wilson, *England's Apprenticeship 1603–1763* (London: Longmans, 1965), pp. 86–87; S. Pollard, *Peaceful Conquest: The Industrialization of Europe 1760–1870* (Oxford: Oxford University Press, 1981), p. 10.
15. The assertion by Dodia that technological change does little to alter the location of agriculture seems overdrawn. Vishay Dodia, 'How Do the Determinants of the Location of Agriculture and Manufacturing Differ?' *LSESU Economic and Social History Journal* I (1) (2019), p. 62.
16. Jones, *Locating the Industrial Revolution* (2010), passim.
17. Mingay, *The Gentry* (1986), p. 57.

CHAPTER 4

Civil War

Another impediment to growth was warfare, which in England since the Norman Conquest of 1066 has always meant civil strife. Damage to life, limb and property was an obvious concomitant, while the associated uncertainty was probably as significant because it dissuaded investors. The classic instance was the Wars of the Roses, which were viewed in old Marxist versions as destroying the baronetage, eliminating the backward 'feudal' elite, and enabling its replacement by more forward-looking individuals. A riposte might be that the landed aristocrats of the late fifteenth and early sixteenth centuries do not strike one as especially progressive; was what happened merely a churning of elite personnel? Economic summaries of the Wars of the Roses are scarce. A modern assessment cites a number of authorities but suggests they concentrate on political and administrative effects and make only indirect reference to economic costs.[1] Documentation is better for the mid-seventeenth-century Civil War, which was physically far more destructive than English legend has it, even if the sources do not dwell on the difficult associated matter of investment withheld.[2] Nor does it seem easy to find clear generalisations about the recovery after 1660, let alone reason to think that any early war spurred more advance in productive technologies—if as much—than might have happened in peacetime.

Strong claims about the cessation of civil wars in England appear in an article by Francis Fukuyama.[3] He reports that after the Norman Conquest the country suffered a civil war every fifty years until 1688–1689, following which there was none. This cycle, he says, was not brought

E. L. Jones, *Barriers to Growth*, Palgrave Studies in Economic History,
https://doi.org/10.1007/978-3-030-44274-3_4

about by rational choice in the form of elite bargaining but by normative developments such as the emergence by the close of Tudor times of a national identity and a strong state, besides during the seventeenth century by a deeper respect for the law. He is sure that this created a context without which elite bargaining of the type involved in resolving medieval conflicts could not have guaranteed stability. The categories and chronology implied by this model may be questioned and it is possible to think that the raw politics of elite bargaining did however remain sine qua non. The enabling conditions, even had they been as strong as proposed, could surely not have ended the conflict by themselves—they had failed to do so in 1640 when elite interests were not very different from 1660. Politics matters.

I shall put forward arguments against Fukuyama's case in order to bias the argument against the significance of removing wars as obstacles. This is a way of assessing the strength of the case and despite cavilling about the means I shall eventually conclude that terminating the cycle of civil war did lift a weight off the economy. War was never cheap and engaging in foreign wars every hundred years or so after the late sixteenth century (with the aim of preventing the coast of the Low Countries falling into any single pair of hands) might be thought to have substituted for the civil war cycle.[4] In terms of tax money such wars were costly—yet they did externalise the damage. Civil war had more directly disturbing consequences and its cessation did reduce expenses. The main hesitation is about Fukuyama's explanation of how the country actually avoided internal warfare after 1660 rather than a suggestion that civil war was not an impediment to growth.

Fukuyama's thesis is structural. Ironically this is the political science equivalent of the deterministic or economistic reasoning which he criticises the late Douglass North for using, although Fukuyama employs less distinct categories. Problems with any theorist's history, economic or political, include taking predetermined abstractions as given; scouting detailed historical experience; and above all disregarding agency. Structural reasoning and historical contingency need to be joined in order to understand the outcomes: they are Siamese twins. The former does put inchoate events into some type of order but the latter exposes the limitations of any purely abstract or conceptual approach.

The notion of a domestic war cycle is suggestive but is vulnerable to hesitations about characterising civil war and identifying 'weak' kings. England's actual experience of political upsets is not easy to fit into the creative hypothesis of a fifty-year cycle. For example, Allen and Leeson's analysis of the adoption of the longbow describes a 150-year window of political stability during the Middle Ages.[5] Similarly the Wars of the Roses rumbled for so long outside the core years of 1455–1487 as to make fifty-year sequences rather arbitrary. It is likely that England's civil wars were less destructive than continental ones yet delving into the history of medieval wars, while interesting, is in truth unnecessary. What is needed is to account for the steep reduction—although not complete absence—of armed conflict after the execution of Charles I in 1649. Fukuyama confines himself to England, regardless that the aim of the early Stuarts was to unite the three kingdoms of England, Scotland and Ireland, the last two of which bore so heavily on events in England that excluding them is scarcely justified.

Were legalism, national identity and the central state in England really enough to prevent recurrences of civil strife after 1649 in the way Fukuyama implies? If risings failed, does that exclude them? Was Monmouth's rebellion in 1685 (termed the last convulsion of the Good Old Cause, though it was not), the rallying behind William III's invasion in 1688 or Bonnie Prince Charlie's incursion in 1745 not at the very least incipient civil wars? The difference is that they were extremely short. But this does not mean that happenstance or the involvement of more compelling individuals than the rash Monmouth, inexperienced Charles Stuart or politically clumsy James II might not have attracted enough adherents to prolong them. As it was, all these episodes threatened the English state. They roiled the financial markets, with capital reported to be in flight to Amsterdam during the '45.

No doubt the break with Rome and adoption of a *Book of Common Prayer* had already conduced to a sense of national, Protestant, identity, but the nation was no unique affiliation. National, regional, county and parish loyalties are not mutually exclusive and were certainly not exclusive in earlier centuries. The question is which came uppermost at which periods? Although the creeping privatisation of strips in the common fields meant that the dominance of parochial communities gradually ebbed, recent scholarship has emphasised the continued role of village memory. There was a long hangover of parochialism which is continually recreated when people grow up together and are not very mobile. By the nineteenth century, when tenanted ring-fenced farms had become the norm, behaviour was less often purely local, yet if loyalties had reached a higher level they often hovered below that of the nation. They could be shaped by the 'custom of the county', which bore on inheritance and the rights of incoming versus outgoing farm tenants.[6] Differences among county customs were not insignificant, a picturesque example being that, when applied to rabbits, one thousand might be understood as 1200! This convention would not have seemed quaint to warreners, who might be quite wealthy men.[7] More significantly and as previously noted written agreements for the letting of farms could be legally overridden by the custom of the county unless this had been expressly excluded. Common usage was sufficient to establish a right that a court would accept.

These practical variations show that even in the nineteenth century national identity had not automatically replaced all else. Other institutions of governance existed and for a very long time the writ of the central government was far from universal.[8] When people like Mary Hyde, mother of the Earl of Clarendon who wrote the classic history of the Civil War, spoke of their 'country', says Alan Everitt, 'they did not mean "England" but Wiltshire or Kent, Leicestershire or Northamptonshire, Cumberland or Durham'.[9] Mary Hyde was the daughter of a clothier in Trowbridge, Wiltshire, who lived much of her life within five miles of a county boundary without once stepping across it. Everitt shows that different counties had some systematically different allegiances during the Civil War and after. This is not to imply there was no nationalism, merely that other loyalties loomed as large in many minds.

Had the state apparatus truly become strong by the end of Tudor times? Overemphasis on the domestic role of the state is partly a reading back from later times when the state had become a Leviathan. Joseph Strayer believed that change was so gradual it is impossible to set a date when loyalty to the state came to dominate.[10] A. J. Pollard concluded that despite Tudor administrative reforms, 'the power of the kings of England nevertheless still remained rudimentary, fragile and ultimately dependent on the assent and co-operation of their subjects'.[11] Well into the seventeenth century, Strayer observed, the best-organised European states were only federations of counties or provinces, each of which adapted orders from the centre to suit its own needs. England was by no means ready to centralise in the 1650s, as the halting rule of the Major-Generals showed. Marked differences in local governance ran across the Restoration divide, implying limitations on direction from the centre.[12]

As to respect for the law, the number of lawyers eventually increased, but sluggishly. During the reigns of Henry IV, Henry VI and Elizabeth laws were passed restricting their number because lawyers were accused of fabricating disputes.[13] Even later, a bill was tabled to exclude lawyers from Parliament, although it was defeated there by the Parliamentarian lawyer, Bulstrode Whitelocke. A degree of difference exists between laws that protect property and the legalism that fosters contentiousness—and provides incentives for lawyers to bring writs. Under Henry VI the tripling or quadrupling of the number of lawyers in Norfolk and Suffolk had been held to be 'to the vexation and prejudice of the counties'. Interpretation was left to the monks, a service that ceased at the Dissolution and was not replaced in some areas until the start of the seventeenth century. At that period it was common for the sons of gentry to be schooled at the Inns of Court. This suggests that knowing how to protect one's interests in the courts was worth the investment in time and money, and that the mediation prevalent in certain regions may not have been a perfect substitute for formal law. Either way, there was no completely dispassionate or reliable legal system. Since corruption reined in the highest reaches the idea that the law was respected, as opposed to being lived with or employed for personal ends, does not square with reality. The law was politicised. Judges during the Interregnum tended to be Parliament men and after the Restoration Charles II appointed judges at the Royal pleasure. Bulstrode Whitelocke and the later Lord Chief Justice, George Jeffreys, scourge of the Monmouth rebels, boasted of the side payments they took.[14] Not withstanding black-letter law England remained awash with cheating that was not tackled until the ending of the 'Old Corruption' in the nineteenth century.[15]

Hypotheses that property had been secure in England almost in perpetuity, or that it was made secure in 1688, or that there was a 'property revolution' during the eighteenth century, scarcely hold water. More to the point, Henry VIII had created some property law to entice purchasers of monastic lands to meet his price, and Charles II felt obliged to ensure some security for people who had bought Royalist estates under the Commonwealth.[16] The fact that private challenges to the ownership of land, though frequent, were not infinite is scarcely evidence of security but may reflect the cost and risk of bringing issues to court. The conventional implication by economic historians that the chief need was security from seizure by the Crown is a little beside the point; the immediate danger came mainly from neighbours or in the case of inheritance, kinsfolk.

Property rights were secure only conditionally; they were contestable. This can be illustrated with respect to land, which for long remained the biggest sector of the economy and possessed much more than rustic significance in the centuries when industry relied heavily on organic, land-based, inputs.[17] Why were rights less than wholly secure? Start with the absence of a land registry, proposals for which were blocked century after century by lawyers whose livelihood relied on writing documents in convoluted language and then charging high fees to interpret them. Private property in land was not unequivocally defined and not freely transferable until the late nineteenth or early twentieth centuries.[18] As will be described in later chapters, old systems of allocating rights decayed only slowly, surviving as vestiges at the present day.[19]

Property law did not evolve in a linear way. Parliament, outfoxed by lawyers among its own members, found its enactments were not invariably carried into effect. Defoe said in 1704 that many laws were not only dormant but had actually been superseded by custom, a reversal of the usual expectation. Local authorities had considerable discretion with respect to enforcement and certain courts could make laws independently of Parliament. There was a marked low in activity in the courts of common law about 1750. Parts of the country managed without the need to take disputes to court and several northern towns lacked more than a handful of lawyers until late dates. The alternative was mediation, witness the tendency of the Quakers (who did not emerge until the mid-seventeenth century) to shun the courts. Legal norms were complicated and seldom set in stone. The fashionable notion, repeated by Fukuyama, that property rights were 'firmly established' in 1689 does not bear much weight, any more than the idea they were hoary with age.

England has a landscape irregular in every respect, with concomitant costs. Comparison between old and newly settled states within the United States demonstrates how difficult transactions are in places where boundaries are not on a grid.[20] In England, titles that lay beyond challenge were at a premium, as is demonstrated by a statement from the Land Registrar as late as 1913 about the astonishing prevalence of incorrect designations. Transaction costs were high, which meant that those with deep pockets could protect what they held but others could never afford the services of lawyers to challenge them. When people below the rank of yeoman did hold copyhold tenure—nominally for three lives—the leases may in reality have been surrendered or renegotiated every ten years.[21] Legal titles and decisions were commonly accepted in practice, but ultimately acceptance was provisional. A leading legal historian gave it as his opinion that, 'establishing rights in privately held land, in the absence of a formal system of registration of title, was a cumbersome matter, both in terms of legal procedure and the evidence required'.[22]

Historians, fixated on relations between lords and kings and by non-market controls as opposed to markets, elevate documentation above practice, just as modern bureaucrats are continually 'tinkering' to tidy up boundaries that were never definite in the first place.[23] In the past, the lack of formal registration meant that ancient genealogies of ownership were recited in the hope of warding off trailing claims. Transactions were attested by long lists of witnesses in the hope of thwarting objections. To establish ownership the testimony of the oldest inhabitants might have to be called on or antiquaries paid to investigate ancient claims. The size and boundaries of fields might be stated in leases and wills using vague terms such as '239 acres more or less', while the ultimately transient trees of the hedgerow were cited as markers.[24] Histories of land measurement tend to celebrate professionalism and overlook antique survivals, yet even today farmers are advised that divisions by hedges and rivers may be governed by little more than the rule of thumb.[25] Uncertain boundaries remain a potent source of argument.

Parish boundaries, tithes, enclosures and field boundaries were all sources of disputes that interfered with investment. Had that not been the case there would have been little need for the practice of beating the bounds whereby a parish safeguarded its right to levy rates. As to tithes, W. E. Tate, doyen of English agrarian historians, said, 'it is impossible in the space at our disposal to enter fully into the not very edifying history of tithes' and he cited the astonishment of a leading agricultural economist 'that agriculture could be carried on at all under such incessant friction as took place between the clergy and the farmers'.[26] Enclosure, too, notoriously led to fallings-out, particularly among members of the elite who had most to gain and the resources to fight their corner.

Enabling conditions like the advancing state or respect for the law were slow to emerge and too weak to ensure lasting peace. They needed raw politics to bring them to life, as is plain from the record of elite bargaining and the individuals and kinship relationships of the persons involved. Participants in the settlements of 1660 and 1688 to 1689 belonged to the same social and economic class. The financiers from the City of London often owned estates and there were cross-cutting relationships and marriages among opposed factions. They shared interests that could only have been harmed by perpetuating conflict. Nevertheless among them were some who were ideological enough to persist in intransigence. Accordingly, it might really matter which individuals steered negotiations that could always have gone awry.

Can one believe that the elite settlements would have been secured by less calculating and more aggressive individuals? Had the participants been different—Monck less canny, Charles II more vindictive or James II less stubborn—it is not fanciful to imagine procedures that would have fanned the slumbering embers of the Civil War. These people had interests of their own and represented wider groups, but they handled negotiations according to their individual psychologies or psychopathologies. Nothing as extreme as a 'great man' theory of history is required to accept a major role for differences in the temperaments of leading figures: Americans might like to consider, as one example, the magnanimity with which Ulysses Grant handled the defeated Confederates and maybe prevented a generation of guerrilla warfare. Charles II achieved a not dissimilar result, witness the 1660 Act of Indemnity and Oblivion which declared an amnesty for (mis)behaviour under the Commonwealth. He permitted many high officials to retain offices they had held under the Cromwells, since their skills would not have been replaceable in short order. A more ideologically committed ruler than Charles II could have tried to manage by staffing every national office with politically reliable men, something that happened in local government, but he was too pragmatic to accept poorer national management or to risk the opposition of those who might have been sacked. They or their sons might have officered a new uprising. Charles was determined to thwart such a possibility in an additional way, by disarming the mob. John Kenyon points out that the confiscation of muskets and handguns from the ordinary people is a little-remarked feature of the Restoration and following years.[27] The return of civil war was made less likely by this act of policy, not by abstract change.

It does not do to de-historicize these things and imagine that structural circumstances could dictate results. Respect for the law, a burgeoning national identity and a strong state, all easy to exaggerate and easy to date too early, might foster peace without guaranteeing it would last. They played a supporting role but, despite Fukuyama's theory, what turned the key in the lock was that regular stuff of politics, elite bargaining. The undeniable outcome was that full-blown civil war did not return and among its blessings, England was spared a resumption of death and destruction.

Notes

1. A. J. Pollard, *The Wars of the Roses* (Basingstoke: Macmillan, 1988).
2. Stephen Porter, *Destruction in the English Civil Wars* (Stroud: Sutton Publishing, 1997 edition).
3. Francis Fukuyama, 'The Last English Civil War', *Daedalus* 147 (1) (Winter 2018), pp. 15–24.
4. C. R. M. F. Cruttwell, *The Role of British Strategy in the Great War* (Cambridge: Cambridge University Press, 1936), p. 1.
5. Douglas W. Allen and Peter T. Leeson, 'Institutionally Constrained Technology Adoption: Resolving the Longbow Puzzle', *Journal of Institutional Economics* 58 (2015), pp. 683–715.
6. William Woodfall, *Woodfall's Practical Treatise on the Law of Landlord and Tenant* (London: S. Sweet et al., 1837).
7. In 1688 Benjamin Stroud, warrener of Aldbourne, Wiltshire, bequeathed rabbits worth £134. Lecture on wills by Julia Hunt, Aldbourne Community Heritage Group, 24 June 2019.
8. Thomas Risse and Eric Stollenwerk, 'Limited Statehood Does Not Equal Civil War', *Daedalus* 147 (1) (Winter 2018), pp. 104–115.
9. Alan Everitt, *The Local Community and the Great Rebellion* (London: The Historical Association, 1969).
10. Joseph R. Strayer, *On the Medieval Origins of the Modern State* (Princeton, NJ: Princeton University Press, 1970), pp. 89–111.
11. Pollard, *Wars of the Roses* (1988), p. 112.
12. Andrew M. Coleby, *Central Government and the Localities: Hampshire 1649–1689* (Cambridge: Cambridge University Press, 1987), p. 233.
13. Henry Moody, *Notes and Essays... Relating to the Counties of Hants and Wilts* (Winchester: Privately Published, 1851), pp. 208–210.
14. Eric L. Jones, *Small Earthquake in Wiltshire: Seventeenth-Century Conflict and Its Resolution* (Sutton Veny: The Hobnob Press, 2017), p. 86.
15. John Wade, *The Black Book, or, Corruption Unmasked* (New Edition, 1829).
16. Eric L. Jones, *Cultures Merging: A Historical and Economic Critique of Culture* (Princeton, NJ: Princeton University Press, 2006), p. 124.
17. E. A. Wrigley has calculated that the land's supply of industrial raw materials and energy for use outside the farm sector rose sixfold between 1300 and 1600 and was two or three times greater than the growth of population. 'The Transition to an Advanced Organic Economy: Half a Millennium of English Agriculture', *Economic History Review* LIX (3) (2006), pp. 435–480.
18. Ron Harris, 'Government and the Economy', in Roderick Floud and Paul Johnson (eds.), *The Cambridge Economic History of Modern Britain, Volume I, Industrialisation, 1700–1860* (Cambridge: Cambridge University Press, 2004), p. 327.

19. For evidence on this and other points cited below relating to the history of property, see E. L. Jones, 'Economics Without History: Objections to the Rights Hypothesis', *Continuity and Change* 28 (3) (2013), pp. 323–346.
20. Gary D. Libecap and Dean Lueck, 'The Demarcation of Land and the Role of Co-ordinating Property Institutions', *Journal of Political Economy* 119 (3) (2011), pp. 426–467.
21. M. A. Havinden, 'Lime as a Means of Agricultural Improvement', in C. W. Chalklin and M. A. Havinden (eds.), *Rural Change and Urban Growth 1500–1800* (London: Longman, 1974), p. 128.
22. Harris, in Floud and Johnson (2004), *Cambridge Economic History 1*, p. 229.
23. Oliver Rackham, *The History of the Countryside* (London: J. M. Dent, 1987), pp. 19–20.
24. Obviously boundary trees could be cut down by the ill-intentioned. E. J. Lainchbury, Jr., *Kingham: The Beloved Place* (Oxford: Alden Press, 1957), p. 17, cites an example from 1659.
25. *Three Counties Farmer*, February 2014.
26. W. E. Tate, *The Parish Chest* (Cambridge: Cambridge University Press, 1969), pp. 136–140.
27. John Kenyon, *The Civil Wars of England* (London: Weidenfeld and Nicholson, 1989), p. 241.

CHAPTER 5

Communal Farming and Underused Land

Release from inefficient methods and underused resources followed no neat chronological path. The most-discussed agrarian change, enclosure, is a prime case, since it took place at various periods in different regions of the country via different vehicles, formal and informal, legal and illegal. The extreme variety of experience is conveniently brought together by J. A. Yelling.[1] An advantage of his study, unusual amidst the huge enclosure literature, lies in emphasising prior, voluntary change within the common fields. One trend, although not universal, was the insertion of more pasture. Yelling shows by means of examples collected from wide areas over long periods how this was achieved.

In short, while agreement to modify common-field farming was obtained more often than the old texts state, it was not invariably forthcoming.[2] The evidence of entrepreneurship trying to force its way to the surface within village communities is almost impossible to sum up but intelligent decisions were reached about sensitive matters, as when the fieldsmen of Kingham, Oxfordshire, used to visit different markets each year to buy bulls for the common herd.[3] This introduced genetic diversity which they undoubtedly assessed by observing the beasts' conformity, as do modern purchasers of livestock. Much would have depended on efforts by the smarter inhabitants to propose and carry out dealings like this. They had only the incentive of expenses for their trouble.

Proponents of adopting higher proportions of grassland or 'new' fodder crops like clover and sainfoin did need to negotiate their way around the institutional stickiness of communal husbandry. Places existed

E. L. Jones, *Barriers to Growth*, Palgrave Studies in Economic History,
https://doi.org/10.1007/978-3-030-44274-3_5

that had made little advance by comparatively late dates. An example was Mere, Wiltshire, in 1791, 'the common fields and common are reckoned dangerous for Sheep in Wet Seasons for want of Draining... and having no Turnips and few inclosed Pastures they usually winter their Lambs out'.[4] Decisions about improving such situations differed greatly, and their timing varied, just as communities and their ecological and market circumstances and the balance of village personalities all differed. Sometimes arrangements were fluid or seem so from our distance in time but on other occasions change was not easily brought about. This gave ammunition to the larger landowners who hankered for the drastic measure of Parliamentary enclosure. As we shall see when discussing how unfamiliar farming practices challenged old entitlements to tithes, new methods and ancient practices tended to be at war precisely because innovations could so easily tend to threaten established institutions. We are seldom party to the debates about such difficulties and altogether know too little about the internal workings of communal husbandry. Yet small-scale farming employed a range of business strategies, such as informal leasing arrangements for livestock and equipment, meaning that relative to large farms it lost fewer economies of scale and did not perform as poorly as might be supposed.[5] This may help to explain the survival in Southern England of so many small farms (measured conventionally by acreage, which admittedly may be misleading) until the mid-twentieth century.

Distinctions between organisational processes and the physical fencing or hedging of land are not always made in the literature, much of which debates the social rather than husbandry consequences of enclosure. Most enclosure histories are directed at one or other of two great waves of activity: the late medieval acquisition of village lands in the Midlands to raise sheep for wool and the Parliamentary enclosures of the late eighteenth and early nineteenth centuries (affecting an even larger central region) which replaced mingled strips with ring-fenced farms. Contemporary and later voices lament the 'sheep eating up men' during the first period and the way small independent farmers were driven into the ranks of landless labourers during the second. Enclosure by agreement receives less attention than Acts of parliament and enclosure by reclamation receives next to none. They are as overlooked as if they were enclosure by stealth, as in truth they often were.

The subject suffers from 'source domination' and topics that offer convenient paper records accordingly dominate what is studied. Lacking dateable information such as Acts of parliament, the process of nibbling away at what was called the waste has typically slipped the historian's noose. Yet several generations ago Hoskins used his familiarity with the ground to show that this was the usual method of land acquisition in Devon, just as the assarting of the woodland had been in counties west or east of the great Midland Plain.[6] Gradual reclamation and the later fencing, hedging, banking or walling of plots taken in from the waste constituted in total a major increase of the farmed area. This land was not exactly being farmed for the first time, since it had typically been employed for low-intensity grazing, but innumerable acres were used more intensively than ever before. Much of the activity took place outside formal markets, perhaps using labour with a low opportunity cost in wintertime, and was intermittent. The sagas of heathland reclamation and the acquisition of other marginal land was on–off over the centuries, with local histories very sparingly detailing land taken in (often surreptitiously, by 'rolling hedges'), abandoned, and recolonized in some later period of expanding population, markets or prices.[7] Grazing more stock on areas between settlements was prone to bring neighbouring villages into conflict. Throughout a long, slow process this encouraged them to demarcate parish boundaries where formality and precision had never seemed necessary before.

Like more conventional forms of enclosure, all this may seem nothing more than a standard 'positive' means of raising output. It may appear to fall within the usual canon and be explained by straightforward responses to rising population, prices or some other incentive. Yet looked at from the opposite point of view, the idle or lightly used acres appear as an impediment in the sense that they had not been fully incorporated in the economic system. Many, perhaps most, of the lands concerned had been lightly grazed 'unimproved' heathland, grassland or woodland. As feed for livestock the quality of the sward was low. Only when improved by the plough and sown with new fodder crops or ryegrass leys could marginal land contribute its full potential to agricultural output and until then it had the makings of a dead weight. Full resource mobilisation was not being attained. Any underemployed factor of production may therefore be seen as a burden weighing on economic life. Under-use dragged down productivity and the conventional emphasis on innovations in institutions and technology capable of drawing resources into maximum use is not wholly misplaced. Nevertheless unincorporated resources count among the impediments frustrating maximum production, as does the diversion of resources into the hands of rent-seekers. The question is where to place the emphasis, whether on the innovations that changed things or on the preceding stage of under-use as a burden in itself.

Notes

1. J. A. Yelling, *Common Field and Enclosure in England 1450–1850* (London: Macmillan, 1977).
2. Yelling (1977), p. 146, gives a wrong impression of some of my observations. Within relatively egalitarian societies some individuals were likely to be pushier than others and to argue successfully for innovation. They did not have to be the ones with the largest shares, though they often were, merely those with the largest personalities. Even so they might not prevail.
3. E. J. Lainchbury Jnr., *Kingham the Beloved Place* (Oxford: Alden Press, 1957), pp. 83, 85. See also J. M. A. Cliffe, *The Husbandmen of Over Norton* (Privately printed, 2011).
4. Quoted by E. L. Jones, *Seasons and Prices: The Role of the Weather in English Agricultural History* (London: Allen & Unwin, 1964), p. 183.
5. Quite the contrary according to Patricia Croot, *The World of the Small Farmer: Tenure, Profit and Politics in the Early Modern Somerset Levels* (Hatfield: University of Hertfordshire Press, 2017).
6. W. G. Hoskins, 'The Reclamation of the Waste in Devon, 1550–1800', *Economic History Review* 13 (1943), pp. 80–92.
7. Sources for this process in Cornwall, Devon and Hampshire are cited in E. L. Jones, 'Enclosure, Land Improvement, and the Price of Capital', *Explorations in Economic History* 27 (1990), pp. 350–355.

CHAPTER 6

Tithes

Tithes were originally one-tenth part of all produce of the land, supposedly paid by farmers as a freewill offering to the clergyman of the parish. In reality the clergy had an incentive to claim tithes as theirs by divine right. As late as 1818, when a Parliamentary candidate in Wiltshire denied the divine right of tithes, the vicar of Devizes had to step into defend this expression of what was, in the eyes of 'the world of orthodoxy', a surprisingly perverse opinion.[1] Many incumbents relied on tithes for much of their income and those who did not were eager to secure what for them was free money. Their sense of entitlement was palpable, as when Rev. William Masters, vicar of Sparsholt, Hampshire, protested in 1812 that, 'Sparsholt is a poor preferment and if I had nothing else, I am sure I could not get mutton and port wine, to which I think every beneficed clergyman to be fully entitled'.[2] Masters' approach was to blame the surveyor, 'Old Thomas Goter', for mis-measuring one of the farms, claiming he was not very accurate 'especially if liquor happened to be in him'.[3] Masters also tried to worm out from an intermediary how much tithe was paid on another farm, saying 'I promise you to keep it a secret'.

Disputes had long arisen because of the complexity of levying tithes in kind on the many types of farm produce, ensuring a host of disagreements about what exactly should be handed from farmer to clergyman. Precisely on which dates the handovers should take place was an additional source of friction, given the variable yields and seasonal nature of farming. Instances of deliberate intransigence were common but one from

E. L. Jones, *Barriers to Growth*, Palgrave Studies in Economic History,
https://doi.org/10.1007/978-3-030-44274-3_6

the tedious and petty array may suffice: about 1732 at Aldbourne, Wiltshire, some farmers used to bring the share of their milk due as tithe in their hog buckets, obliging the vicar to pour it out for his hogs since it was unsuitable for any other purpose.[4] At the same time, the vicar's man used to go round with a bag collecting tithe apples. To settle conflicts about onerous and fraught procedures of this type, requirements were increasingly imposed by legislation, although the stipulations were less than comprehensive and tended to be dispersed through case law. Lawyers were the most obvious beneficiaries from the courtroom wrangles about precedents. Further exacerbating the practical and legal difficulties was the unwillingness of farmers who were not communicant members of the established church to contribute towards funding its functionaries.[5] Their reluctance was matched by grievances on the side of clergy who thought they were losing out when farmers argued that plants hitherto unfamiliar as field crops should not be included among titheable produce.

Lord Ernle began the chapter on tithes in his classic textbook of agricultural history by asserting that tithes were 'a serious obstacle to the progress or recovery of agriculture'.[6] He went on to point out that tithe owners were 'sleeping partners in the cultivation of the soil', contributing neither capital nor labour but demanding part of the produce. The burden had perhaps been more or less accepted when farming remained stationary—slow-changing is what this must mean—but when husbandry practices began to alter 'the grievance was acutely felt' and the imposition of tithes on their enterprise depressed the incentive for farmers to invest. If things went well seats in the church might be reserved for farmers who paid tithes. Arrangements like this were disturbed by more rapid change during the late eighteenth and nineteenth centuries and the history of tithes became more fraught than before. Unquestionably, tithes were likely to impede innovation and waste resources in disputes until the Tithe Commutation Act of 1836 reassigned the burden.

The point about discrepancies between old institutions and a more rapid pace of change is scarcely ever made in work on tithes, an exception being the explicit remark by Anthea Jones that 'changes in agricultural practice could obviously cause dispute: tithes were suited to a static agricultural system'.[7] She illustrated this by a 1772 case at Broadwell, Gloucestershire, where a farmer cropped a pasture but claimed the previous pastoral exemption from tithe should still apply. Anthea Jones further noted in a book on the history of English parishes that 'when land use changed or new crops were introduced a sharp question about tithes immediately arose'.[8] Parliamentary enclosure was an especially likely source of upset, since an increase of production was expected and tithe owners hoped to secure a share of the gain. That there was a general relationship between agricultural change and tithe disputes is further supported by Fernand Braudel's observation that in the eighteenth century the French clergy tried, but failed, to levy tithe on improved pasture or 'artificial meadow', i.e. improvement after the English fashion.[9]

Abolishing the payment of tithes in kind, which was the purpose and effect of commutation, was a major advance. They had been so costly and contentious to gather that they had commonly been negotiated away by the end of the eighteenth century, but that was precisely the time when other occasions for conflict were emerging. The intensification of agricultural development after about 1750 put unprecedented pressure on established arrangements. For farmers to avoid paying tithes on unfamiliar crops and previously minor practices undermined the clergy's expectation of sharing the full product of the land. Incumbents were inclined to insist on the letter of their ancient rights but were not so wedded to tradition as to refrain from trying to extend them when farming became more profitable (strictly, more intensive). By the 1790s some Suffolk clergy were surveying their whole parishes to aid tithe collection.[10] Clergymen also objected to retrograde moves in the countryside like imparking, when landowners replaced productive farmland with leisure grounds, a fashion that further reduced society's full use of its resources.

Disputes multiplied on two fronts, one because cultivating less familiar crops prompted farmers to dismiss any liability for paying tithe on them, and the other because the agistment of livestock journeying to more distant markets also encouraged farmers to avoid paying tithe. (Agistment was when animals were fed on someone else's land for a fee.)[11] Court cases involving agistment increased greatly during the third quarter of the eighteenth century. This is not surprising since in London and many other towns the population was growing, which given relatively inelastic demand for food may be taken as a rough-and-ready index of the market for meat and other livestock products. During the first half of the eighteenth century London's population had risen rather little but it rose from fewer than 700,000 in 1750 to 900,000 by 1800 and over 1,600,000 by 1830. The rise in demand persuaded farmers to grow plants that were unusual as field crops, largely for the purpose of feeding animals. It also multiplied movements of livestock across the country to the swelling urban meat markets. This gave some farmers the opportunity of specialising in agisting animals that were en route, paying or not paying a tithe on the proceeds of this business almost as they chose. Details of the livestock trade were supplied in 1797 by James Mathews, *Remarks on the Causes and Progress of the Scarcity and Dearness of Cattle...*[12] Mathews insisted that prices had risen steeply since 1760. In his view demand was outstripping supply, although he interpreted it as a reduction of supply.

Widespread dissatisfaction among the rural population led eventually to the Tithe Commutation Act. Its solution of buying-out the tithe owners was expensive—they received generous compensation in the form of land—but removed an everyday source of dispute and assuaged what had been an enormous source of friction in the rural economy. Paying the tithe in cash was unwelcome but was less costly and less aggravating than managing the tricky calculations of liabilities in kind or fighting over the dues in court. Nevertheless, the tithe charge continued to spark resistance from parishioners who were opposed in principle to supporting the established church.[13]

During the eighteenth century tithes were no longer solely local affairs. They could be bought and sold and had often become commoditised. There were 'tithe farmers' who had bought the right to tithes as income-bearing property and constituted a class of proprietors distinct from those parish incumbents who depended on tithes for their living although inclined to band with them to protect their mutual rights. The clergy themselves were faced with especially difficult problems that often led them to fall out with uncooperative parishioners: first, as we have seen, because the 'small tithes' owed to them were costly and cumbersome to collect. It often involved monitoring and gathering tiny fractions of minor agricultural products. Secondly, the farmers resented tithes as irritating costs and saw efforts to extend their scope as taxes on enterprise. During the Last Labourers' Revolt of 1830, farmers even spotted the chance to blame tithes for their inability to pay higher wages. The classic case was at Selborne, Hampshire, where the mob was apparently spurred on by the farmers to demand that the vicar reduce his tithes. The consequent riot, during which the workhouse was destroyed, led to some of the labourers being transported to Australia.[14]

Most of the attention in a rather thin literature is devoted to conflicts over the tithing of crops, some of which (especially potatoes and swedes) were being grown increasingly for livestock feed during the second half of the eighteenth and first half of the nineteenth centuries. Historians pay less attention to the parallel friction resulting from increased stock movements, which deserves better treatment. Admittedly nothing was strictly new about claiming tithe for animals fed in more than one parish: the patterns of property ownership, family relationships, ecological differences from place to place, and the vagaries of weather or season meant that some movement of livestock had always taken place. Customs grew up about them, for instance that the tithe wool belonged to the incumbent of the parish where the sheep had been wintered. The fact that expectations varied from one locality to another did not help to settle matters when agistment was increasing.

London's drawing power reached far afield and offered farmers along the routes stretching from Scotland and Wales or the West Country a profitable chance to agist animals. This was evident in a dispute at Whaplode in the Lincolnshire fens, a parish that the incumbent, Rev. Thomas Bateman, made conspicuous by long-winded, detailed and angry pamphlets condemning his parishioners for not paying agistment tithes on the large numbers of animals halting there on passage to London.[15] His case became widely cited. When he came to the parish in 1768 he had found parishioners fattening large flocks of sheep and cattle before sending them on but failing to pay a tithe for the privilege. The men whom Bateman took to court admitted trading and feeding livestock in transit but claimed either that they had never heard of agistment tithes or that these had never previously been levied, at least on animals kept in the parish for less than one month or for sheep which had been sent on before they had been sheared. Confusion reigned. Resort to the law cost Bateman dear and he did not win outright. In the neighbouring parish of Holbeach the vicar had already issued a similar challenge in 1768, the report about this in Rayner's *Cases at Large Concerning Tithes* (1783) being taken from a pamphlet called *The Nature of Agistment Tithe of Unprofitable Stock*.[16] ('Unprofitable stock' was a husbandry term, not a commercial one, and meant animals not kept for ploughing or milking.)

Disputes about agistment became common as the reach of London and other markets extended and grew in scale. But stress on existing tithe arrangements was most visibly exerted by the more widespread cultivation of less familiar field crops. In 1787 Henry Heathcote, rector of Walton, Lancashire, advanced his claim to tithe potatoes with the unusually explicit declaration, 'that he was activated by a need to preserve the profit of his living in a much changed agricultural situation… the articles I am pursuing at present are such as did not exist to any degree of consequence a very few years ago. Viz. Agistment and pasturage of unprofitable cattle that is of horses not kept for the plough… of sheep from their last shearing, of Butcher's cattle & of cows that are agisted for hire & not milk'd in the parish'.[17] Apparently these classes of livestock were being fed partly on potatoes.

What helped to bring the issue to a head was a conflict at East Meon, Hampshire.[18] In 1826 the parish had acquired a fresh vicar who, in the way of new incumbents, felt his enormous income was inadequate.[19] He wished the tithe rate, traditionally ten per cent, to be raised to twenty per cent and its scope extended to swedes, which (because they were resistant to frost) had become the mainstay of winter sheep feed.[20] In 1831 he prevailed in court against a member of a local elite family who had stepped forward to defend the farmers' interest. A little earlier a comparable case had been brought at Lichfield, Staffordshire, whose incumbent wished to bring cabbages, also being used for sheep feed, within the scope of tithing, while cases involving potatoes, formerly less familiar as a field crop, had become numerous during and after the late eighteenth century. Extending tithes to swedes or cabbages, which were inputs to the fattening of titheable sheep and cattle, would have been double-dipping, an unacceptable principle that had been noticed long before but was ignored or overlooked by the court in the East Meon case.[21] Two years after that case the brother of the farmer's unsuccessful champion, who happened to be an MP, was however able to persuade Parliament to rescind the verdict. Following several attempts, the Tithe Commutation Act was passed soon afterwards.

Disputes might be expected at any time of innovation and rising product prices, because it was then that tithe owners had a motive for seeking a share of the extra rents. Conflicts might therefore have been anticipated in the late seventeenth and early eighteenth centuries, when four separate sources relating to Surrey, Buckinghamshire and Dorset noted regional shifts in prosperity created by the introduction of clover and other fodder crops: 'The innovations, concentrated on the uplands, were a threat to the economic position of the heavy land farmers, who must formerly have agisted beasts for their Chiltern neighbours, and indeed the price of permanent meadow fell in many places'.[22] Concomitantly the innovations raised relative incomes on light land. Spells of generally falling prices, on the other hand, disadvantaged farmers at large who might then have been expected to deny liability for tithes. This assumes that their costs did not straightaway fall in the same proportion as receipts, although had they done so, 'loss aversion' would undoubtedly have ensured that few farmers would have admitted the fact. They were caught, or believed they were caught, in the lag between costs and revenues. Unfortunately secondary sources on tithes are not presented chronologically and it is not easy to trace a distinct pattern of disturbances before the late eighteenth- and early nineteenth-century upsurge of conflicts about potatoes, swedes and agistment. At that period the disturbances are patent and in an article I likened them to pouring new agrarian wine into old institutional bottles.[23] Tithes have been summed up as reducing rents on arable land by 25 per cent and on pasture and meadow between 14 per cent and 17 per cent.[24] Lifting so weighty a burden was clearly worthwhile but could not be managed smoothly or cheaply when different interests contended. Parliament had to step in as tiebreaker.

Notes

1. *Wiltshire Archaeological and Natural History Magazine* 104 (2011), p. 226.
2. Letters re tithes in the Heathcote Collection, Hampshire Record Office, 18M54/C1/1/21, Box H E No.1-6. I am grateful to Stephanie Albery for transcribing these and other documents.
3. Within the pages of a book labelled Sparsholt Tythes is a note on a scrap of paper, 'Thomas Goter's evidence criticised adversely by Wm. Master in letter to Sir Wm. Heathcote 16.7.1813 as being unreliable in memory and frequently drunk'. Full disclosure: Thomas Goter was an ancestor of mine.
4. Transcribed Aldbourne deed number 113 seen by courtesy of Julia Hunt.
5. See e.g. the disputes in which the rector of Camerton, Somerset, engaged with a parishioner who was a Roman Catholic. Howard and Peter Coombs (eds.), *Journal of a Somerset Rector 1803–1834: John Skinner* (Oxford: Oxford University Press, 1984), esp. p. 187, referring to 1822.
6. Lord Ernle [Rowland Prothero], *English Farming Past and Present* (London: Heinemann and Frank Cass, 1961 [1912], 6th edition), p. 332.
7. Anthea Jones, *The Cotswolds* (Chichester: Phillimore, 1994), pp. 147–148.
8. Anthea Jones, *A Thousand Years of the English Parish* (Moreton-in-Marsh: The Windrush Press, 2000), p. 150.
9. Fernand Braudel, *The Identity of France II* (London: HarperCollins, 1990), p. 281. I am indebted to Shaun Kenaelly for this reference.
10. J. A. Theobald, 'Changing Farm Sizes in Woodland High Suffolk, 1690–1840', *Proceedings of the Suffolk Institute* xl (part 1) (2001), pp. 55–64.
11. Eric Jones, 'Livestock Movements and Agistment Tithes', *Southern History* 40 (2018), pp. 116–133.

12. James Mathews, *Remarks on the Causes and Progress of the Scarcity and Dearness of Cattle*... (London: Scarlett and Nunn), 1797.
13. Disputes involving religious acrimony as late as 1901 are illustrated by those between the church and Methodist farmers at Hemyock, Devon. See Brian Clist, *Make Hay While the Sun Shines* (Blackdown Hills AONB: 2009), Chapter 2, 'The Tithing Affair'.
14. J. L. and Barbara Hammond, *The Village Labourer II* (London: Longmans Green, 1948 edition), pp. 61–62; John Owen Smith, Selborne and Headley Workhouse Riots of 1830 www.johnowensmith.co.uk/om/htm accessed 4 July 2019.
15. Thomas Bateman, *A Treatise on Agistment Tithes* (London: Privately printed, 1779, 2nd edition). The first edition appeared the previous year.
16. *Rayner's Cases at Large Concerning Tithes* (London: Richardson and Urquhart, 1783), p. 659.
17. Eric J. Evans, *The Contentious Tithe: The Tithe Problem and English Agriculture: 1750–1850* (Milton Park: Routledge Revivals, 2017 [1976]), pp. 46–47.
18. Michael Blakstad, 'The Tithing of Turnips—A Hampshire Village in the Westminster Spotlight' (East Meon History Group website).
19. Blakstad calculates the incumbent's receipts from tithes in 1852 as £232,830 at 2016 prices.
20. E. L. Jones, *Seasons and Prices: The Role of the Weather in English Agricultural History* (London: Allen & Unwin, 1964), pp. 122–123.
21. Henry Gwillim, *A Collection of Acts and Records... Respecting Tithes* (London: Privately printed, 1801), I, p. 227, quoted a medieval judgement that 'one land shall answer but one tithe for one year, and the agistment is but the profit by the mouths of the beasts of the same land'.
22. E. L. Jones, 'English and European Agricultural Development 1650–1750', in R. M. Hartwell (ed.), *The Industrial Revolution* (Oxford: Basil Blackwell, 1970), p. 60 and n. 1.
23. Jones, 'Livestock Movements and Agistment Tithes', *Southern History* 40 (2018), pp. 116–133.
24. Evans, *The Contentious Tithe* (2017 [1976]), pp. 99–100.

CHAPTER 7

Archaic Institutions

As Lord Ernle made clear, tithes were an unequivocal burden on farmers, an extreme case of rent-seeking by the clergy. Nor were tithes the sole arrangement impeding a productive allocation of resources: communal agriculture was another obvious and almost countrywide example. It has died the death now, apart from rare vestiges like the open-field village of Laxton, Nottinghamshire, and an occasional manorial court leet convened or revived to deal with infringements of managerial by-laws.[1] The argument might be made that the inefficiency of communal agriculture in strictly economic terms was accepted because society had other goals. These included maintaining approximately equal access to resources, which involved permitting the community's animals to graze the common fields after harvest, and sustaining the resource indefinitely. Securing agreement to plant and fence off innovative crops was hard, so all told the system might have been thought a device for preserving equality in principle and poverty in practice.

The time-horizon of villagers and small farmers was longer than many interpretations allege and was perhaps infinite in principle. Yet they did pay some attention to raising output within the communal system—such as the purchasing of bulls, previously mentioned, or the slowly successful adoption of new crops. Chief among adverse interpretations of their behaviour is the notion of the 'tragedy of the commons' proposed by the biologist, Garrett Hardin, in one of the most-cited journal articles ever.[2] Despite refutation, his view has sunk deep into the public consciousness. Hardin had not researched or even read agricultural history

E. L. Jones, *Barriers to Growth*, Palgrave Studies in Economic History,
https://doi.org/10.1007/978-3-030-44274-3_7

and blithely asserted that, because each individual commoner had a hypothetical incentive to overstock, he or she would do so. Hardin assumed that people would cheat and as a result degrade the commons. If this were so, it is not clear why terminal degradation had not occurred during the Middle Ages.

In reality, manorial regulations of great intricacy limited grazing rights and protected the resource. That instances of overstocking by greedy men did occur cannot be gainsaid but they were protested against and resisted.[3] The exception seems to have been Holland Fen in Lincolnshire where there was said to have been no limit to stocking and seemingly enough feed for Scottish drovers to get away with clandestinely putting on sizeable numbers of their own beasts.[4] That seems highly unusual. Hardin might have had a defensible case over non-agrarian resources, such as the exploitation of marshland birds and birds' eggs, where some species were driven to extinction on England's side of the North Sea. Neither he nor as far as I can tell his critics mentions this weakness of communal organisation. Some of the extinctions were however externally inspired. They were brought about by rich sportsmen collecting specimens or rare eggs or paying villagers to do so. English villagers were not casual about more central agricultural resources but were nevertheless barely able to protect them against enclosure, which could involve rent-seeking, impure and simple. The Acts of Parliament which abolished the common fields assigned disproportionate shares of the land to handfuls of rich proprietors and clergymen, while Tithe Commutation allotted still more. In a narrow sense all this was lawful but in many parishes so much of the common fields was moved into private hands that the pre-existing system was crippled. On the truncated areas left to them small farmers could scarcely maintain communal agriculture.

Evaluating enclosure is tricky. In terms of physical output, the subsequent farm economy was able to produce more food and agricultural raw materials (leather for example) to supply the vastly growing nineteenth-century population. By itself, communal agriculture may have supplied each village adequately but was probably unlikely to have created a growing surplus and done so well by the buyers of bread in the cities. To that extent, shrinking the old system did correct underperformance. How onerous the defect may have been is a matter of nuance and judgement and depends on whether assessments are meant to compare England with other countries at the same date or with its own past. Change over time in England is the present focus and in that respect the country's overall performance was creditable. Governments had long been alarmed at the prospect of famine or rather at the social disorder it might bring. Nevertheless Restoration parliaments were already confident enough to spur the export of grain by means of bounties. Self-interested the parliamentarians may have been, because many of them had an interest in high prices for the cereal crop, but they were right, or fortunate, in that the problem was eliminating itself: the age-old scourge of famine petered out early in the eighteenth century.

What share of the growth of output really did result from enclosure is unclear. The seemingly logical approach via time-series correlations between Acts of enclosure and wheat yields is unpersuasive. It assumes that the larger post-enclosure farms raised output because they achieved economies of scale. But increased output after the mid-1830s rested on complementary inputs of artificial fertiliser and machinery and it is uncertain how far enclosure was needed to bring them into play. We may be misled by the fact of enclosure into attributing too many of the gains to it. The case that only the larger farmers could afford machinery and that broad acres alone would have enabled it to be deployed, an argument once advanced with great confidence, ignores the emergence of a rental or leasing market including 236 proprietors of machines by 1861. Agriculture as an industry was more flexible than it appears: small farmers could hire machines and engineers for short periods without incurring the capital cost of purchase.

Traditional institutions for denoting ownership and use-rights or to allocate resources may certainly have worked against maximising production. The absence of overarching institutions to determine ownership (and therefore grease the wheels of the market) was hindrance by default. In short what mattered was not solely developing new arrangements but clearing away old ones. Devised to protect traditional claimants, old dispositions could thwart alterations that might have created a consumer surplus. An Act of enclosure was a means of cutting the Gordian Knot even if its distributional consequences were unkind as a result of tossing the land of a parish into a pot from which the most powerful owners could extract the larger shares.

An example of inefficiency was the notorious failure to establish a Land Registry, an institution with plenty of foreign precedents. While 'drag' might be a better term, sloth in the institutional sphere represented an inherent tendency to resist progress. In England all ranks of the legal profession, up to and including the law lords, rejected proposals for a Land Registry that would have reduced the fees charged for their expensive and sometimes interminable manoeuvrings. They were successful century after century. In the absence of public registration, titles to land had to be signalled by long chains of deeds or by 'shepherd's memory' about occupation, ownership, boundaries and rights of way. Identifying and securing rights was so important that in some parishes semi-official or unofficial registers were kept to record transactions in land. For example, at the end of the sixteenth century the justices of the peace ordered a calendar of this sort to be made for several of the hundreds in north-central Hampshire, while at Fairford, Gloucestershire, there survives a volume of documents about mortgages, assignments and wills from the 1590s to the 1670s.[5]

Ordinarily, expensive lawyers and courts were needed to advance or defend claims of ownership. In some parts of the country—an outstandingly varied country of course—there were substitutes for law that amounted to mediation by independent local assessors, but in complex matters this was not always conclusive. Formal law eventually took over. It was understandable, but damaging, that resort to the law had lagged; going to court was a costly business, giving the advantage to owners who were already rich and could 'wear out' their challengers.[6] The effect was greatly to raise transaction costs, as it still does: disputes over boundaries remain endemic. Country solicitors say that old deeds may still prove valuable for some purposes and we have noted that Parliamentary enclosure documents are occasionally consulted about routes and boundaries. And as also noted, the fifteenth-century judge, Sir Thomas Littleton, wrote *Tenures*, which was treated with nothing short of reverence by Sir Edward Coke, leading jurist of Elizabethan and Jacobean times. *Tenures* was long regarded as the principal authority on real property law and was still cited in the courts during the twentieth century.[7] Such things are not all mindlessly antiquarian, they can matter. Unlike Australia or Canada, where the state grants exploration rights, it is common in parts of England for one person to own the land surface and someone else to own the land beneath. Mineral rights can date back hundreds of years to the old manorial rights of large landowners and the church, and can be retained when the land is sold. The country has large deposits of zinc and lead, hence it may not be surprising that the present-day Church of England has asserted its rights over more than half-a-million acres.

Reforms and amendments of common-field routines were sluggish and intermittent, depending on what rate of change one expects. At first the market made what must surely appear as only plodding headway in breaking up Walter Bagehot's 'cake of custom', but it did make headway. The Benefactions Board in the church at Stanford-in-the-Vale (then Berkshire, now Oxfordshire) records that in 1764 two bequests were amalgamated and used to buy eight acres in Wantage Field, which were rented out and the income used for the original charitable purposes. Moreover, it is possible to find a gradual sale of common-field stints divorced from the properties to which the rights originally related. Stints became commoditised. Towards the end of the seventeenth century the rights of commonage at Calne, Wiltshire, had already begun to be detached from the houses to which they had originally belonged.[8] After selling a house in 1787, a barber surgeon, presumably meaning a well-to-do doctor, was permitted to retain its beast lease (the right to graze a beast). Ownership of the beast lease no longer obliged him to undertake the duty of watch and ward. From that untraditional permission granted to someone with influence it was no great step to making beast leases marketable commodities. One that was sold in Calne in 1742 entitled a much later purchaser to a plot in the common fields when they were enclosed in 1812.

More widely, outside investors were already buying parcels of farmland. A fraction of the middling farmers were moving into trade. The great estates bought up their farms, monopolising whole districts. One defect of this monopoly was the 'tragedy of the anti-commons'—Heller's term, the opposite of Hardin's—whereby strategically placed individuals could frustrate change over considerable areas.[9] An alternative term is 'group exclusion', although a single person could block change. Further frustration came from intra-elite conflict, where disputes or foot-dragging over the division of the spoils delayed a number of enclosures, probably more of them than are known.[10] Nor was it only elite individuals who dragged their feet over innovation. In the early seventeenth century freeholders in general were inclined to oppose anyone who wished to form enclosures within the common fields. They were fearful of losing land on which their animals might graze. Later in that century, when sainfoin and ryegrass were more prevalent, the old fears are said to have been allayed by the greater availability of feed.[11] The introductions were usually the province of the larger farmers and we may anticipate that the smaller men were still reluctant. Reasons for thinking so include the partial and gradual adoptions of a whole variety of 'new' fodder crops, accompanied by the frictions that surrounded the intrusion of unfamiliar techniques into communal arrangements. But, as in eighteenth-century Calne, restrictions were softening over time.

Another instance of the market spreading in the teeth of old ways is tithes. They were commoditised in that non-resident proprietors had often bought the rights. These tithe owners joined forces with resident clergy to try to maintain the system whenever they could not readily extract a good share of any receipts from innovation. They definitely succeeded in extracting large shares of the land in return for eventual commutation. Old methods of organisation therefore lingered for a long time, as the shreds linger today. Many are at their final gasp, although a tiny handful of traditional institutions continue to operate. Historically, reform could be thwarted at the highest level or even find itself reversed. It has long paid the legal profession to defend antique methods. Oliver Cromwell tried to reform the Court of Chancery in 1655 but it survived scandalously unchanged into the nineteenth century. The Restoration succeeded in halting constitutional and legal reform.[12] Charles II restored the Rotten Boroughs. England's institutions favoured the incumbents and there was no 'growth programme' to override them of the type that might have been adopted by an authoritarian ruler such as Peter the Great.

Another ancient institution, once almost ubiquitous in the urban and manufacturing sectors, was the guild. In modern times, guilds survive less usefully, where they survive at all, as dining clubs and occasions for ceremony. But for centuries craft guilds and borough guilds regulated the quality, price and volume of goods produced, and the number of participants in a given trade or who were permitted to establish their businesses in a town. Newcomers were excluded or charged a high entry fee to become freemen of the borough. Economies of scale were limited by restricting the size of businesses, most notably via a ceiling on the number of apprentices each craftsman might take. Potentially, guilds safeguarded consumers against substandard or overpriced goods, which was a meritorious function, but by the same token they ground producers down to the one level. It was the businesses and incomes of guild members that were being protected. Guilds were anticompetitive, sharing the market among their members. They resisted technological change. Stability rather than enterprise was what they prized. The ability of borough governments to suppress enterprise is probably revealed by the fact that southern towns remained on the whole under conservative management whereas Midland and northern towns often lacked that type of control and were more likely to grow. Even in the South the seemingly regressive guild system was slowly but surely undermined. Guild members defended their practices during depressions but (although this is difficult to document) matters were seemingly let slide in boom times, when work was available for all.[13]

Other broad forces acting to circumvent guild regulations may be mentioned. One was the late medieval and early modern rise of rural domestic industry, primarily cottagers with looms in their dwellings. Their costs were low because they were located in the countryside. Free from the charges imposed by borough jurisdictions, the looms could divert some family labour to manufacturing in the intervals of agricultural work or it could make work for the unemployed. This 'ruralisation' was a large-scale movement that undercut the guilds. Another force was the steady shift of production from the long-established industries of the south of England to weakly regulated northern and West Midland towns. In yet another direction, guild jurisdiction was given the slip in London where, despite official attempts to limit the capital's size, producers set up in the suburbs. In London a member of one trade guild was entitled to take up another trade, which created a flexibility not associated with the stereotypical guild system. The power of the city guilds was actually dismantled in the wake of the Great Fire of 1666, when the need for numbers of carpenters and building workers was urgent if reconstruction were to take place. The Fire Court overrode restrictions on the entry of skilled workers from rural areas.

Most interesting of all and least tractable was the shift in elite opinion in favour of using the judicial system rather than settling disputes by personal violence.[14] In 1599 judges ruled that confiscating goods during searches by guild officers was illegal. At the very start of the seventeenth century guilds were losing cases they took to court with the aim of compelling incomers to enrol as freemen. A ruling to this effect in 1616 became a common-law precedent and few town guilds could afford to resist in the courts. The legal powers of the guilds were eroded: indeed the whole system was subject to erosion from the late sixteenth to the nineteenth century. We must assume that the judges were close to the entrepreneurial ethos of the metropolitan trading community and more willing to support its norms than those of producers in small provincial towns. Given the atmosphere of corruption in the courts, judges or their families may have been compromised by investments in the productive and trading branches of the economy. As a result of their increasingly pro-business mood, the encumbrance of the guilds slowly evaporated.

In celebrating England's progressive elements we should not minimise the sloth and struggle that beset market expansion. It is possible to imagine the country as exhibiting what C. R. Hallpike called the 'survival of the mediocre'.[15] Mediocrity in this sense means the survival of practices that would have been eliminated in more competitive markets: their long, slow replacement, with occasional survivals right up to the present day, does need explanation. Limited markets in which old-fashioned allocative and technical practices were sheltered from competition provide the most general one. Markets were kept small by widespread poverty, undeveloped communications and no doubt the preference of many a producer for a quiet life.

Economic historians are inclined to dwell on development. Their mindset, taking its cue from market economics, is to think primarily about innovations that actively increased the social product. If there had been stasis, everything would have been in equilibrium and economists, practising an equilibrium science, would become interested only when growth upset it. Sir Henry Maine spotted the *deformation professionelle* of the economist in 1861. He wrote that, 'the bias indeed of most persons trained in political economy is to consider the general truth on which their science reposes as entitled to become universal, and, when they apply it as an art, their efforts are ordinarily directed to enlarging the province of Contract and to curtailing that of Imperative Law…'.[16] Market exchange thus occupies the economist and modern economic historian, the inner workings and obduracies of older societies organised by custom or status being brushed aside. Market inducement is thought so powerful that the dissolution of obstructions is taken for granted. Scholars can certainly give the impression that the diffusion of inventions was smooth and paper over the difficulties, particularly when they write broad histories. Dutton and Jones criticised this tendency on the basis of their close study of the pin industry, stressing the uncertainties of the market and the role of interpersonal relations between contracting parties.[17]

The slow retreat or replacement of institutions such as guilds, tithes and communal farming is reminiscent of the grand interpretation by the arch-institutionalist, C. E. Ayres. He envisaged the motor of history as the milling of institutions by technical change, a concept not unlike Veblen's distinction between technology and ceremony or even Maine's distinction between status and contract.[18] In Ayres's elaboration of this canon, technology is the exogenous variable. Institutions do not adapt fast enough to match technological change. Besides the deeper puzzle of what caused technology to advance, which he leaves aside, there was another that his model seems too general to explain, i.e. the fact that institutional decay occurred at such different rates. Sociological and anthropological approaches seldom come to grips with inconvenient features of history like this, which is not to say that we can turn to writers of empirical history for an explanation. Historians offer ad hoc interpretations rather than employing a consistent structure of generalisation. Combining the approaches appears desirable.

Communal farming fits Ayres's schema fairly well, although it has to be recognised that what he proposes is very general and reminds one of a reference he makes to what Hobson said about Adam Smith, which is to say that Smith's system is a baggy one assuming its shape according to where it is picked up. Nevertheless Ayres's proposition makes sense. For centuries, techniques and crops altered little in communal agriculture. In the minds of historians the big alteration was enclosure, mostly taken in the literature to signify Parliamentary enclosure. But this was preceded by informal and formal agreements to privatise some of the land. The opportunity was seized to adopt 'new' crops distinct from the common rotation, which can be formulated as a technical change challenging old modes of organisation. Enclosure made those decisions redundant.

Enclosure restricted access to the land and therefore to its yield of natural products. Poorer members of village communities resorted to supplementing their diet with what was called 'famine foods'.[19] Gleaning was open to all after harvest unless and until the larger farmers began to confine access to the wives and families of their own workers. Otherwise village people sought berries, fruit, mushrooms, nuts and other wild foods. In upland parishes where the land had fallen into a few hands they desperately sought anything that might heat their houses, even stubble, beech leaves or twigs fallen beneath rooks' nests. Farmers encouraged them to hunt species like house sparrows to make 'vermin pie', which was acceptable to people short of protein and simultaneously reduced agricultural pests. Much of the scrabbling for natural resources was done by women and children whose labour had a low opportunity cost.

Unlike systematic studies of 'famine foods' in continental countries, the English situation is little understood. The wild species gathered can be listed and mentions found of the search for them but we do not really know how much protein was acquired like this, when or where. It was a distributional matter of importance to village communities, but this does not necessarily speak to the dietary health of the entire population.

The problem may have been generated or intensified by shifts in the locational centres of gravity of cropping and eighteenth-century population growth. Conceivably the growth of poverty arose in a 'welfare gap' between the cessation or waning of monastic and other religious provision for the poor and the increase in living standards ultimately achieved by the nineteenth-century economy but for the moment this can be only supposition.[20]

Equating the trends of national output, which are not well understood, and those of Parliamentary enclosure is unsafe, even leaving aside the complication that the area affected by enclosure Acts was limited. The south-east corner of the country, the far north-east and all down the western side of the country were largely unaffected. Nor were those who acquired extra land as a result of enclosure under any obligation to farm it, certainly not at once and not necessarily by the latest methods. A ready supply of capital for land remodelling and additional inputs was not guaranteed. To dwell on the point, the customary attribution of gains to enclosure may to some extent be a case of *post hoc ergo propter hoc*. There are data on wheat yields which might be used as a proxy for total output but they are unsuitable as an index of the effects of enclosure, not least because in 1800 a substantial part of the British population lived on cereals other than wheat.[21] Recent calculations of wheat yields show the steepest gains from 1820 to 1850 and suggest that changing rotations, husbandry routines, new crops and regimes of drainage may have been more important, playing a role only indirectly dependent on enclosure.[22] This reinforces the case that improvements were neither certain on land affected by Parliamentary enclosure nor confined to it.

Turning to another great institutional topic, the decline of the guilds, this proves more amendable to an Ayresian approach. The reason is that despite some case law removing guild powers, no decisive break took place like the enclosure of whole parishes or the reorganisation of tithes. Viewed over the long term, the guilds just faded away. Economists would dismiss Ayres's theory as no theory since all it does is allude to a recurrent lag between ill-defined technical and institutional changes. It is too broad. Even so, for all its lack of power to predict the timing of events (also a fault of standard economic theory), Ayres's notion of institutions milled by technical change is applicable in many quarters. It does offer a framework. Its utility is supported in that he knew nothing about guilds, tithes or common-field farming yet his schema is transferable to them. At least he is not contradicted by history in the way Hardin is.

A similar guarded appreciation might be offered of Hallpike's 'survival of the mediocre' thesis. Criticism is hesitant rather than dismissive because the idea does offer another framework for the slow decline of old institutions, as well as of minor industries in the south of England, neither phenomenon having attracted much scholarly notice. Hallpike's work had the merit of being based on fieldwork. Unlike Ayres's conjectural history, his analysis was based on observation of tribal societies. He concluded that inefficient practices were not selected out by a Darwinian process, as his fellow anthropologists thought. He noted the fetishising of items so bizarre they cannot have been selected to maximise well-being, such as the worshipping of an eclectic variety of animals or occasional natural features arbitrarily picked out of some purely local array. This hardly refutes evolutionary selection since all it says is that the context barely permitted it to work: much of the world's population lived for millennia in small groups lacking contact with others or exposure to competing religious or other ideas. Penetrated by more coherent theologies from the outside, subsumed it might be said in larger markets, local beliefs could sometimes be swept away, although in parts of South-east Asia Buddhism and Islam are still contending with rather resistant spirit worship.[23]

Hallpike showed that evolutionary process was not universal. Conditions had to apply before it could operate, that is societies must become sizeable and connected enough to promote competition. He does not specify thresholds beyond which societies actually do become big enough for competition to eliminate local beliefs. We might surmise that the residue of arbitrary ideas, e.g. the little ender–big ender disputes about religion and so forth that still disfigure the world, tended to derive from the clashing beliefs of whichever groups happened to come uppermost when smaller populations were conquered and converted. Such beliefs may lead to inefficiencies at the national level, including warfare or the persecution of minorities, without being strong enough to suppress economic growth. The assumption by some neoclassical economists that institutions must be optimal or they would be eliminated by Darwinian-style competition is challenged by the enormous spectrum present at any one moment.[24] Institutional evolution required decades and centuries to work itself out, a time scale not envisaged by proponents of optimality.

In a search for an operational theory, we may return to Hardin's tragedy of the commons and Heller's contrary hypothesis of a tragedy of the anti-commons. The first may be dismissed as unhistorical. To share out and preserve the common-field system, villagers regulated themselves and their fellows and did not automatically overstock the commons. On the other hand, 'anti-commons' points to an observable phenomenon, the process of group exclusion whereby small groups or single individuals could frustrate an innovation desired by others.[25] Intra-elite conflict, a failure by the larger owners to agree, for instance on how to carve up the spoils of enclosure, was a difficulty that was only gradually overcome, partly by a fresh calculation of costs and benefits by new generations of owners. The catch with this approach is that it is primarily descriptive and lacks predictive power. It takes the form that change can take place when no-one insists on standing out, whereas if even one strategically placed person does object, change may be blocked. Parliamentary enclosure may be seen as one means of overcoming objections because it was set up to permit the owners of a majority of the land area to dominate the remainder. Without being able to force the issue in this fashion, individuals with small stakes in the common fields had typically been slow to agree on changes in rotations. Who among the villagers would take which position can best be investigated case by case; a neoclassical maximising assumption will not explain the varied behaviour seen. Nevertheless the structure of communal farming acted to slow down the wheels of an optimal allocation of resources, viewed, that is, from the standpoint of maximising physical output.

In a model that attempts to unify the declines of guilds, tithes and communal agriculture, market expansion is exogenous. It is sufficient for the present to note that the eighteenth- and nineteenth-century market was expanding and colliding with existing modes of organisation in one sphere after another. Whereas traditional institutions retained ample power to obstruct or delay, England's economy was loosely textured enough for growth to take place in its freer corners. Ancient restrictions persisted but increasing numbers of people were persuaded to by-pass them. Their success heightened the competition whose rewards had seduced the ambitious in the first place, without eliminating each and every antiquated practice. Growth predated the machine age.

Notes

1. E. L. Jones, 'Economics Without History: Objections to the Rights Hypothesis', *Continuity and Change* 28 (3) (2013), pp. 323–346, details long-lasting survivals of several types.
2. Garrett Hardin, 'The Tragedy of the Commons', *Science* 162 (1968), pp. 1243–1248. Compare Jones, *Locating the Industrial Revolution* (2010), pp. 218–220. Hardin eventually returned to the topic but again offered no historical research and did not seriously modify his position, while nothing has dampened the enthusiasm of his numberless followers. Garrett Hardin, 'Extensions of the Tragedy of the Commons', *Science* 280 (1998), pp. 682–683.
3. J. A. Yelling, *Common Field and Enclosure in England 1450–1850* (London: Macmillan, 1977), p. 156.
4. James Sandby Padley, *The Fens and Floods of Mid-Lincolnshire* (Lincoln: Privately printed, 1882), p. 49.
5. E.g. Walter Money (Introduction), *Of All the Lands... Viewed...1595* (Newbury: W. J. Blacket [date illegible]); the Fairford Booke, copy in the possession of Fairford History Society.
6. This manoeuvre was explicitly noted of Francis Popham of Littlecote: www.links.org/links... Francis Popham.
7. Maxwell Fraser, *Companion into Worcestershire* (London: Methuen, 1949), pp. 113–114.
8. A. E. W. Marsh, *A History of the Borough and Town of Calne* (Calne: Robert S. Heath, 1903), p. 79.
9. M. Heller, *The Gridlock Economy* (New York: Basic Books, 2008).
10. Eric L. Jones, *Locating the Industrial Revolution: Inducement and Response* (Singapore: World Scientific, 2010); Chapter 10, 'The Pace of Change'.
11. Frank Emery, *The Landscape of Oxfordshire* (London: Hodder and Stoughton, 1974), p. 109.
12. John Kenyon, *The Civil Wars of England* (London: Weidenfeld and Nicholson, 1989), pp. 245–246.
13. For details of guild decline see Jones, *Locating the Industrial Revolution* (2010), pp. 101–104.
14. J. R. Kellett, 'The Breakdown of Gild and Corporation Control Over the Handicraft and Retail Trade in London', *Economic History Review* 10 (3) (1958), p. 381.
15. C. R. Hallpike, *The Principles of Social Evolution* (Oxford: Clarendon Press, 1986).
16. Sir Henry Maine, *Ancient Law* (London: J. M. Dent & Sons, 1917 [1861]), p. 179.
17. H. I. Dutton and S. R. H. Jones, 'Invention and Innovation in the British Pin Industry', *Business History Review* LVII (2) (1983), p. 193.

18. C. E. Ayres, *Theory of Economic Progress* (Chapel Hill: University of North Carolina Press, 1944). As with theories of this type the choice of exogenous variable is arbitrary and once chosen all else is made to devolve from it.
19. The extent to which famine foods might be relied on by the European poor is best exemplified by marginal environments in the Alps. R. A. Dodgshon, *Farming Communities in the Western Alps* (Springer Nature Switzerland AG, 2019).
20. E. L. Jones, 'Economic Adaptability in the Long Term', in Tony Killick (ed.), *The Flexible Economy* (London: Routledge, 1995), pp. 79–110.
21. E. J. T. Collins, 'Dietary Change and Cereal Consumption in Britain in the Nineteenth Century', *Agricultural History Review* 23 (2) (1975), pp. 97–115.
22. Jose L. Martinez-Gonzalez et al., 'Building an Annual Series of English Wheat Production in an Intriguing Era (1645–1761): Methodology, Challenges and Results', *Historia Agraria* 79 (Dec 2019), pp. 1–29, especially graph 3, p. 17.
23. See Tom Harrison, *World Within: Borneo Story* (Oxford University Press, 1984), on the overwhelming success of Christianity.
24. Kausik Basu et al., 'The Growth and Decay of Custom: The Role of the New Institutional Economics in Economic History', *Explorations in Economic History* 24 (1987), pp. 1–21.
25. Jones, *Locating the Industrial Revolution* (2010), gives examples.

CHAPTER 8

Obstructive Infrastructure

The history of small-scale firms and institutions is obscure. A lack of records for small businesses means that rather few have been studied and those that have are not unequivocally representative. Practices that were taken for granted at the time escape scrutiny. Minor improvements in office work, say, or warehousing or transportation are overshadowed by the attention given to better-recorded sectors of the economy, large organisations and compelling technologies. The impression nevertheless abides that productivity gains came from unsung advances in a sprawling mass of little enterprises, despite the treadmill of dreary routines that may also be found. By contrast with these 'soft' changes in organisation, physical infrastructure is visible; local historians tend to be aware of it and discuss how it evolved. Its prominence means it can be studied.

Did physical obstructions represent serious costs or were they so readily replaced as not to hinder development? Different vintages of construction mark phases of economic growth and it may be thought that buildings were continually renewed as growth took place. Buildings were certainly replaced when rising incomes or rising prices made it likely to be profitable. Take agriculture: farms were remodelled during times of boom, such as the Golden Age of agriculture in the 1850s and 1860s, only for many of the buildings to be abandoned in the twentieth- or twenty-first centuries, when farming came to be carried out with tractors rather than teams of horses. The landowners and big farmers who had invested in altering layouts must have found their standing barns and existing equipment hampering what were in those times the latest methods.

E. L. Jones, *Barriers to Growth*, Palgrave Studies in Economic History,
https://doi.org/10.1007/978-3-030-44274-3_8

The temptation is to assume that replacement was automatic, that when gains might be expected from a new edition, as it were, the requisite effort and investment were forthcoming. This is reminiscent of the 'vasty deep' problem, alluding to the Shakespearean remark that spirits may be called from the vasty deep but may not come. It is unlikely an immediate response was forthcoming, with no lag before structures of a new vintage were put up. The assumption of a speedy response is unwarranted because old structures may have been too costly to replace or were restored by owners emotionally attached to buildings they had always known. The opportunity cost of retaining them may have been borne more or less willingly, despite the fact they were in the way of newer versions. It is merely a neoclassical hypothesis to think every opportunity would be seized. Cash was necessary for expenditure but cash alone was not sufficient. In his study of Yetminster, Dorset, Machin discovered a correlation between high product prices and the rebuilding of farmhouses but he pointed out on the basis of deep research that scarcely known changes in the tenurial policies of landlords were probably as important in accounting for the timing and quality of new building.[1] On those grounds, price history alone is unlikely to explain the phases of construction.

Nor can it be said that building was something taking place on a blank sheet. Developments were shaped by features anciently incised in the landscape. These legacies, entangled in the baffling obscurities of property law, were capable of diverting subsequent plans. The historical setting was astutely recognised by Barrie Trinder.[2] He saw that industrial sites such as the mines, factories, canals, railways and towns of the eighteenth and nineteenth centuries could not be divorced from the history of a long-settled countryside. They were shaped by boundaries established under the seven Anglo-Saxon kingdoms, medieval monastic estates, burgage plots laid out in the bastides (planned towns) of the twelfth century, and common land that had remained unenclosed because the lordships of manors were fragmented in the Wars of the Roses. The distribution and chronology of development had to adapt to mixtures of history, law and topography.

It is in their layouts, rather than the appearance of their buildings, that settlements most perpetuate their former selves. The antiquated condition of buildings is somewhat misleadingly emphasised. Hundreds of studies by vernacular architectural historians have been made of old buildings, which are often patchworks and not as old as they look, but comparatively few exist of the probably older layouts of the settlements. Buildings are immediately obvious and can be aesthetically appealing but layouts are important too. Narrow, winding lanes and interlocked properties imposed extra transport and distribution costs that can persist as dead weights on the economy even today; in the past communication networks quickly became choked by what in modern terms were thoroughly minor increases of traffic. Where multiple owners were involved, some of them rearing to restart their businesses as soon as possible after a disaster such as a settlement fire, they commonly deemed the exchange of property too vexatious. This applied especially in towns and large villages where ownership was dispersed among small tradesmen. To judge from the legacy of crooked streets and cramped house plots in English towns, the costs of negotiation were even higher than when enclosing the open fields.

Rivers are surprisingly convenient locales for addressing the history of construction. They provided resources such as route-ways, fish stocks and water power which were important to many groups, but at the same time rivers could be barriers. Impediments to river trade came in two forms, man-made obstructions such as weirs and mills and natural obstructions such as shoals or the awkward coils of river courses. Take the former. The vested interest of millers protested that the removal of weirs would damage mills which depended on the power of the water impounded behind them or more often that any reduction in transport costs would attract produce from a distance and bring loss to local producers. Farmers argued that making riverside markets more accessible would attract suppliers from further afield and undercut sales of their own crops. Fear of import competition was thus the commonest argument, although—as a pretext—both local monopolies and farmers were prone to put the threat of flooding first. Disputes boiled down on one side to representations advanced by urban merchants who imported grain, besides the consumers of bread, and on the other by farmers nervous about lower-cost producers gaining access to 'their' markets. Further opposition to river improvement came from many sides, including waggoners who could not match the low prices of waterborne transport. All these factions made a great noise but, by and large, were overwhelmed by the interests of growing towns. Plainly, however, urban interests could not prevent some schemes for clearing the waterways being delayed or abandoned. After all, laws had been passed since 1066 against creating obstructions in rivers. The fact that similar enactments appeared time and time again in the following centuries is a sign that little was really done to keep waters free for navigation, one reason being that much local law enforcement was under the control of fishery owners.

Physical obstacles, whether natural or constructed, had to be dug or blasted out of the way (shoals) or dismantled (weirs). This could be managed, as far as pre-machine engineering allowed, but needed the consent of others with rights in the watercourses, including the fishermen who sold fish bred behind the weirs. Complaints and protests against interventions were legion, although the foremost student of the subject, T. S. Willan, cites many a chapter and verse for the fact that when formal objections were carried as far as Parliament they stood a good chance of failing.[3] As usual there was more than one side to any question and the multiplicity of interests in rivers might mean that Acts of improvement were less propitious than they seemed. They commonly incorporated clauses forbidding straightening channels or building new wharves. The anticompetitive atmosphere created by the overlap of so many scarcely compatible interests was palpable. Improvements were achieved but, as Willan concluded, the restrictions attached to them had to be looked on as the price for getting Acts passed and could amount to 'serious handicaps'.[4]

Turning to look at rivers from the opposite viewpoint, as barriers rather than corridors, there is little evidence about how they were first crossed—by ford—except as remotely signalled by place names, such as Oxford, Wallingford or Fairford. The earliest bridges have gone too, having been made of wood that rotted away. Provision had often been monastic, as on the Thames at St. John's Bridge, Lechlade, and after the Dissolution towns were inclined to establish religious guilds to continue the maintenance of their bridges.[5] Maintenance costs for wooden bridges could be high and a historian of Weymouth, Dorset, was puzzled that stone from nearby Portland was not used there instead.[6] She overlooked the technical problems. Large stone archways were too difficult to build at first and their weight necessitated massive abutments which restricted the flow of water. The transition from wood to stone tended to await the late eighteenth century. Until then, whereas gaps could be left in wooden bridges between the piles or via drawbridges inserted to let barges pass, similar passages were hard to make through stone bridges. The problem was dealt with only when denser traffic inspired the needed engineering effort.

The variety of competing interests created delay, expense and confusion in dealing with the man-made problems of weirs, mills and bridges and the physical problems of shoals and convoluted meanders. During the sixteenth century a complicated tussle about the sharing of harbour dues between the Dorset towns of Weymouth and Melcombe Regis delayed for decades building a bridge between them.[7] The twin boroughs sat virtually cheek by jowl because Edward the Confessor had given the monks of Winchester the land on the opposite side of a narrow stretch of water from Weymouth, where Melcombe Regis was to develop. This shows how transport provision, comparatively straightforward in itself, might be held up by the most ancient dispositions. Common sense agreement would have saved both sides money; economists might expect the differences to have been settled by bargaining. In practice, once conflict had started, it became progressively more tribal and embittered. Legal remedies were possible but were abnormally slow and expensive. At length, the Privy Council lost patience with the two boroughs and knocked their heads together to make sure a bridge was built.

Belated change can also be illustrated from the Oxford district. Until 1769, when Swinford Bridge was opened to replace a ferry over the Thames at Eynsham, Oxford had no satisfactory access from the west.[8] Farmers bringing their produce to Oxford market were obliged to unload their waggons and transfer the goods to packhorses at the western end of what is now Botley Road. The modern Botley Road was then called Seven Bridges Road, an indication of the multiple engineering tasks and investments required to tackle the problem. A new causeway was needed. With the aim of providing a fresh carriage road along this route from Wales and Gloucester to London, the effort was finally made by linking the improvement of Seven Bridges Road with the Earl of Abingdon's building of Swinford Bridge. Investing in a carriage road from the west sturdy enough to accept commercial as well as passenger traffic (as long as both paid tolls) was a sign of rising prosperity. Completion of the entire task owed much to the labours of the prominent lawyer, Sir William Blackstone, which was a tribute to the managerial skill needed, not least to overcome the factitious resistance of the senior common room of Christ Church, Oxford. Blackstone himself thought the law too sluggish. The Earl of Abingdon became a local monopolist, since no other bridge was permitted within three miles of Swinford Bridge. The perquisite of the toll makes it still a valuable property in the twenty-first century and the County Council lacks the funds or power to abolish it.

Higher up the Thames, stone bridges had been built from the twelfth century and several continue in use in the twenty-first century. They were put up in locally available stone and the small arches which were all that medieval masons could readily manage were wide enough for the minor craft of the shallow upstream reaches. This is a further demonstration of physical constraints on trade, although what the history of rivers chiefly tells us is that the most intractable problems came when physical and institutional difficulties reinforced one another. Eighteenth- and nineteenth-century bridges were partly financed by tolls and records sometimes survive of the revenues collected. In other respects the study of early bridges, roads and much else in the field of communication is like archaeology, which is to say that physical remains are to be found but little is known about their use. We can see the surviving objects and their architects may be identifiable but the volumes, composition and value of traffic are matters of conjecture, making the early history of the subject more like the work of morticians than of physicians.

Many stone bridges were over-engineered, not that early engineering can be wholly dismissed. We have only to contemplate the erection of Salisbury's tall spire (in the same county Malmesbury's main spire did admittedly fall down) or the ingenuity of river commissioners to admire the sophistication that could be exercised at distant periods. To give one instance: the commissioners appointed in 1608 to determine whether a rebuilt mill on a tributary of the Kennet in Berkshire was interrupting the flow to downstream mills closed the new mill's gates 'and sett up an howre glasse' to time how long it might take to block the flow.[9] That was quite experimental. Unfortunately science did not yet extend to calculating stresses. Rather than have a bridge collapse, medieval engineers were likely to build it more massively than would now be thought necessary. Later Robert Hooke calculated the stresses in high walls and tall buildings, besides building the Monument to the Great Fire of London (202 feet high and additionally intended for experiments), but it is not clear how fast such expertise was diffused or as far as bridges were concerned how strongly the need was felt.

The Middle Ages left an inventory of bridges capable of bearing the traffic of the years between 1540 and 1770.[10] Away from the outskirts of London, additional bridge building was limited throughout that long period. Does this really mean that the stock of bridges was sufficient for the late pre-industrial economy? Perhaps so: for a long time no general complaint about congestion is heard and, as with the proliferation of medieval churches, there may have been over-servicing. The conclusion may be that there was enough capacity to accommodate the relatively minor increase in the volume of land transport until the pressures of the mid-eighteenth century spurred increased provision. Yet this conclusion may be a little bland. Responses to changing demand were neither automatic nor instantaneous. Not everyone agreed instantly to invest in new structures. We can surmise that bridge capacity was hard-pressed for a few decades during the mid-eighteenth century and for a time stood somewhat in the way of economic expansion.

The examples of Melcombe Regis and Weymouth, and of Swinford Bridge, indicate the delayed provision that could arise in the forms of obsolete roads, narrow bridges, dangerous ferries, and away from the physical sphere, vexatious institutions. It is almost surprising that so many rivers were successfully canalised and bridged, and made suitable for trade, but late eighteenth-century growth swung the balance. The growth and industrialisation of Georgian times produced loads that were too heavy for wooden bridges and techniques were then developed to replace them in stone or iron. One study estimates that over eighty per cent of major medieval bridges were demolished between 1770 and 1830.[11] This marks the key phase of growth when bridges were replaced because they were inadequate for heavier wheeled traffic. The author of the study suggests that fashion also played a part, thereby acknowledging the customarily underplayed role of amenity preferences.

Eighteenth-century advances in surfacing imply that road provision was becoming inadequate for the traffic. Although some defects of road surfaces were put right quite early, this is obscured by the habit of neglecting all signs of improvement in favour of concentrating on turnpike trusts and the numerical data they provide. An Act of 1691 already gave parishes the power to levy a highway rate. The need is to show that traffic was held back by too few or too poor roads, rather than believing that better communications were generated the instant growth made them seem worthwhile. Before the adoption of wheeled vehicles from the end of the seventeenth century, travelling conditions were probably adequate for existing purposes.[12] After the Restoration, as London grew, the vastly increased movement of sheep and cattle towards the capital, or the fattening pastures around it, was accommodated by drove roads like the Ridgeway which crossed the downs and wolds. Pepys and Evelyn both travelled throughout Southern England in four- or six-horse coaches without coming to harm. Dramatic accidents involving coaches date from the early nineteenth century and exaggerate the poor state of the roads. What caused accidents was mainly bad weather. It was the advent of large numbers of wheeled vehicles that damaged the surfaces of the old roads and started the switch to better surfaces.

Until demand became truly pressing a lag in providing better roads was likely. Meetings had to be held, capital raised and bills put before Parliament. Eric Pawson points to an anomalous downturn in the formation of new turnpike trusts during the 1770s and suggests that capital and effort may have been diverted to competing projects like enclosures and canals.[13] The problem was therefore a shortage of capital for all the projects that the late eighteenth century might have desired. It is reasonable to suspect that a consequent lag in the provision and improvement of communications may have been responsible for holding growth back for two or three decades.

Occasional early town walls and gates of stone are still to be seen, for example Bargate in Southampton and Westgate in Winchester, but the roads have by-passed them and they stand islanded as curiosities. The memoirs of James Spershott at Chichester record the taking down of a tower in 1781 and part of the wall in 1809.[14] That was not uncommon. The medieval fortifications, already redundant, may have become comforting again as defences during the Civil War but afterwards they were simply a nuisance. Most towns cleared them away when traffic was growing. How serious an obstruction they had become—how long they delayed development and what effort was needed to cope—no doubt varied according to local circumstances. But in general the eighteenth century saw a surge in the demolition of urban obstructions.

German bombs and English developers have done their best to expunge the built past. For all that, remnants in the form of old buildings and the persisting layouts of towns, not to mention unimaginably ancient boundaries and routes, all survive in astonishing numbers. The tourist industry depends on them. The attractiveness of surviving market towns and villages is testimony to municipal sluggishness and the absence from rural areas of the rapid growth that replaces antiquities with more up-to-date structures. The South to North shift of industry may suggest that capital as well as labour leached away from the south. The question is, did the buildings that were left behind interfere with further development or were they by-passed in favour of regions with more active investment?

One answer is found in the manner whereby land ownership cramped urban expansion. The classic case appears in W. G. Hoskins, *The Making of the English Landscape*, and concerns Nottingham.[15] The city had been outstandingly attractive in the seventeenth century but had since become 'a squalid mess'. The urban area was tightly held in the grip of its open fields with their multitudinous strips and the right of common pasturage over them. The burgesses who owned the pasture rights refused to permit enclosure, despite the wishes of freeholders in the fields and despite anguished wrangling over the politics involved. As a result men built on every scrap of land inside the field area and when none was left they built upwards. The town became grossly overcrowded and insanitary. Only in 1845 could the reformed corporation force through an enclosure and let the town burst onto its open fields, but as Hoskins says the damage had been done. Nottingham was now a by-word for back-to-back slums not cleared until the mid-twentieth century. Property rights which the lawyers could not unscramble and only government could override were the culprits. The burgesses were not entirely villainous, since they were merely small men protecting themselves, but their behaviour had cramped the town.

Nottingham was not the only town to experience the chafing of the new against the old. Consider St. Ives, Huntingdonshire, which for 750 years was hemmed in on the east by large estates once owned by Ramsay Abbey and St. Ives Priory but passing at the Dissolution into new hands which saw no advantage in erecting houses on their land.[16] They were rich enough not to seek profits from development, which reinforces scepticism about the galvanising effect of the Dissolution, and indicates the harm done by great inequalities of wealth. St. Ives was much smaller than Nottingham and its ownership pattern did not generate slum building in the same way but it could expand to the east only when the Slepe Hall estate was broken up after the death of the owner in 1847. On that date there were takers for the land. St. Ives arose from its 750-year torpor and began a modest growth.

No one had anticipated growth on the scale of early industrial times, which finally forced the reorganisation of so many sectors of the economy. The sequence of change varied. Equipment was sometimes upgraded without obvious fuss, for instance the water mills of Worcestershire were mostly rebuilt during the late eighteenth century, an exception being the mill of about 1620 at Churchill which was supposedly too substantial to be easily demolished. On occasion change could beat fruitlessly against established arrangements for a long time but the case that obstructions interrupted widespread growth relates chiefly to the third quarter of the eighteenth century.

Industrial growth also struggled within the straitjacket of old property rights held by men who (or whose wives) had enough cash to maintain a taste for scenery amidst the seductions of entrepreneurship. In 1781 in

Dorset the Sherborne silk manufacturer, William Willmott, had to bribe the man controlling water levels to get enough power for his mill, since the landowner's wife did not like to see the level of the pond fall.[17] He was put to the expense of installing a horse mill to assure power for half the mill, effectively an insurance that was technologically a backward step. And in Derbyshire the cotton spinner, Richard Arkwright, was obliged to restore a stream to its course in order to protect the Duke of Rutland's corn mill and trout fishing.[18]

Reality on the ground therefore partly disposes of a solution favoured by economists, that is to say substitution. The simple remedy would have been for an entrepreneur to move somewhere more congenial to his business, substituting one plot or set of premises for another. On the face of it there were ample opportunities to do so and we know that men did move, a famous example being the shift of the lacemaker, John Heathcoat, from Loughborough in Leicestershire to Tiverton in Devon. Few manufacturers were so mobile. Additionally, the variety of England's geology, overlain by its jigsaw of property rights, thwarted many a plan to engage, say, in mining or quarrying in situ. Landowners and entrepreneurs in Southern England tried and tried again to find coal that either was not present or lay so deep their shafts could never reach it. In the south, enterprise and capital were, so to speak, cast on the desert air. Reality's lucky dip favoured other geological provinces and located the mining industry in the Highland Zone. Power, like minerals, was important too, and in early industrial times fast streams were needed for power: once again the fates favoured the high rainfall, hard-rock areas of the north and west. Only steam was in principle footloose but steam, too, was favoured by the unequal distribution of coal measures capable of fuelling the engines cheaply.

Approached in the broad, therefore, we sometimes find industrialisation blocked or diverted not merely by unequal property ownership and amenity preferences but by natural distributions of resources. Two views of this found sharp expression in Marxist theology. One school played up the possibilities and limitations inherent in the natural world, the other (powerfully proclaimed by Stalin) urged that the human spirit was always capable of overcoming the deficiencies of nature. This sounds like an extreme version of substitution but some substitutions are out of the question and Stalin was just wrong. He would certainly have been wrong about the English economy, which was obliged to adapt slowly and painfully to the distributions presented by real-world geology.

Nor was it always possible to find substitutes at the local level. Take the situation in Nottingham. A hypothetical argument might be made that if industry were blocked there it could always have moved elsewhere. After all, Leicester, which was not far away, did not suffer the indignities forced on Nottingham by its stubborn burgesses. And some entrepreneurs did relocate over considerable distances, as when glass making shifted from Gloucestershire to Newcastle or early cotton manufacturing went from Lancashire to Derbyshire. But that is to take too Olympian a view. Local capital was owned and populations distributed in ways that meant manufacturing was seldom so footloose. In Nottingham most businesses continued to accept the cost of remaining. This may be taken as a final demonstration that tradition, inertia and barriers did play a role in what might be called the crooked timber of the industrial revolution. The funds needed to solve the problems were forthcoming though not always straightaway; there does appear to have been a brief hesitation in investment during the third quarter of the eighteenth century, precisely when trade was expanding. It may have been sufficient to cause a hiccough until antiquated barriers could more readily be overthrown.

Notes

1. R. Machin, *The Houses of Yetminster* (University of Bristol Department of Extra-Mural Studies, 1978), p. 156.
2. Barrie Trinder, *The Making of the Industrial Landscape* (Gloucester: Alan Sutton, 1987), p. 5.
3. T. S. Willan, *River Navigation in England 1600–1750* (New York: Augustus M. Kelley, 1965).
4. Willan, *River Navigation* (1964), p. 53.
5. David Gordon Wilson, *The Making of the Middle Thames* (Bourne End, Bucks: Spurbooks, 1977), p. 88.
6. Maureen Weinstock, *More Dorset Studies* (Dorchester: Privately printed, n.d.), p. 38.
7. R. R. Sellman, 'The Dispute Between Weymouth and Melcombe Regis', in Weinstock, *More Dorset Studies* (n.d.), pp. 5–20.
8. E. de Villiers, *Swinford Toll Bridge 1769–1969* (Eynsham History Group, 1969).
9. Eric L. Jones, *Revealed Biodiversity: An Economic History of the Human Impact* (Singapore: World Scientific, 2014), pp. 94–95.
10. D. Harrison, *The Bridges of Medieval England: Transport and Society 400–1800* (Oxford: Oxford University Press, 2004).

11. D. Harrison, 'The Fate of Medieval Bridges Since 1770: Demolition, Survival and Presentation', Proceedings of the Institute of Civil Engineers: English History and Heritage Virtual Library 166 (1) (May 2015), pp. 45–54.
12. C. Cochrane, *The Lost Roads of Wessex* (London: Pan, 1972), pp. 112–114.
13. Eric Pawson, *The Turnpike Trusts of the Eighteenth Century: A Study of Innovation and Diffusion* (Oxford School of Geography, Research Paper 14, 1975), p. 30.
14. Francis W. Steer, *The Memoirs of James Spershott* (Chichester: City Council, 1962), pp. 23–24.
15. W. G. Hoskins, *The Making of the English Landscape* (London: Hodder and Stoughton, 1955), pp. 218–221.
16. Bob Burn-Murdoch, *The Shaping of St. Ives* (St. Ives: Friends of the Norris Museum, 2009), pp. 71–76.
17. Maureen Weinstock, *Studies in Dorset History* (Dorchester: Privately printed, 1953), p. 92.
18. M. H. Mackenzie, 'The Bakewell Cotton Mill and the Arkwrights', *Journal of the Derbyshire Archaeological Society* LXXIX (1959), pp. 62–64, 74.

CHAPTER 9

Maladministration

Compared with what would have been possible, England was badly administered in the centuries before industrialisation. Inefficiencies are not hard to find. Consider the Royal Proclamation of 1615 which banned the use of wood fuel in the manufacture of glass, spurring the move to coal-fired glassworks in Newcastle dedicated to producing luxury glassware. The monopoly closed down the small wood-burning furnaces in the south that had made cheap glass. Protectionism is perennial, as Adam Smith was to show. A plausible justification can always be found for putting special interests ahead of the common weal. The ostensible reason for the glass-making monopoly was to protect the supply of timber for building ships, an appeal to national security which was thought beyond demur. A similar patriotic duty was advanced from time to time by other nation states in Europe.

In England, monopolies granted during the Stuart period were broken up but Georgian parliaments continued to be congeries of interest groups and remained vulnerable to special pleading, as when the East Midlands' hosiers secured the Tewkesbury Act of 1765, outlawing that town's annoyingly cheaper manufactures. The apparent paradox is that neither governmental favouritism nor the convolutions of contemporary law entirely halted industrialisation. In the eighteenth century, rent-seeking was on a slow decline, besides which some special interests may have cancelled one another out. At the very start of the century Mandeville had written that, 'Every Part was full of Vice, Yet the whole Mass a Paradise'.[1]

E. L. Jones, *Barriers to Growth*, Palgrave Studies in Economic History,
https://doi.org/10.1007/978-3-030-44274-3_9

Not quite every desirable change awaited the nineteenth century. Some improvements did come early. Censorship, for instance, had been enforced by law and before that by direct action, as with the public burning in 1683 of *A Treatise of Monarchy* (1643) by Philip Hunton (Cromwell's choice as first provost for the aborted Durham College). Ridding the land of such intemperate measures and then of censorship laws was a see-sawing affair but was achieved as early as 1695. Just how effective censorship had actually been is unclear because seventeenth-century London printers had avoided it by putting out work to Edinburgh. During the eighteenth century, a range of thoroughly different impositions on economic life were tackled piecemeal. The scourge of smallpox, for instance, was circumscribed by voluntary endeavour in the shape of inoculation and then via Jenner's pioneering of vaccination, which was imitated from place to place. In the sphere of street lighting local efforts provided the answer. The gains from illumination by gas (though of particular advantage to prostitutes) were plain enough for it to be quickly adopted by town authorities. The improvement of urban layouts and traffic circulation was another achievement of the eighteenth century.[2]

Private and voluntary efforts were however rarely enough. Medical interventions such as the introduction of iron hospital bedsteads were not always generalised, while suppressing corruption required the hand of the state and the force of the law. Only the Quakers stood self-consciously aside from public dishonesty. In the countryside, many villages remained under rigid landowner control or their communal farming was unduly restrictive but many small towns were smartened up, even while their manufacturing was leaking away to larger ones. After about 1800 factory wages may have flattened the distribution of income a little (an opinion hotly contested) but factories tended to be localised and over the country as a whole the first gains were probably eaten up by population growth.

Thorough-going institutional change—truly immense change once it did arrive—awaited the reformist years between 1830 and 1850. Initiatives then came thick and fast. With the Reform Act of 1832, and even more with the Municipal Corporations Act of 1835, the ice was broken. The metaphor catches the spirit of G. M. Trevelyan's rendering: 'At last the ice-age of English institutional and corporate life had come to an end, and the life of the community began to be remodelled according to the needs of the new economic society'.[3] Benthamite questions about social utility took hold, quizzing one venerable absurdity after another.

The extent of distortions is revealed by the reforms adopted to tackle them, as the following catalogue shows.

The Reform Act had signal effects, including making a start on shifting political power from southern agricultural areas towards northern cities. This is not to say that every reform was as radical as its proponents might have dreamt. Shocking as some innovations were to the conservative mind, the process was Fabian rather than revolutionary. As late as 1867 over half of the MPs remained connected with the land. Trevelyan, quietly sympathetic to the society being born (properly cautious, because as a historian he contrasted it with what was being replaced rather than with what followed), saw merit in the Reform Act's very circumspection. He thought this persuaded the upper classes to stay in politics and prevented the emergence of a class of professional politicians concerned solely with their own advancement. But upper-class participation meant the Corn Laws could still be defended and the entry of dissenters into Oxford and Cambridge resisted. Deference persisted and as Asa Briggs concluded, 'tradition was a brake on progress'.[4]

One index of an inefficient distribution of resources is the extent of corruption. An operational definition is rare in the historical literature, but neither the corrupt practices of Georgian public life nor their shrinkage in early Victorian times can be in much doubt. During the eighteenth century, national office was seen as the route to private gain, any sense of the public good being conspicuous by its absence, but the 'Old Corruption' was brought to heel in the nineteenth century. An unruly society in which even cabinet ministers had gone armed in broad daylight was substantially tamed. Growing public distaste at corruption offered support, although achieving reform involved tedious political manoeuvring and clashes of personalities. Day-by-day change was intermittent and can be too readily telescoped into a smooth trend. Moreover, the elimination of evils did not occur purely from affection for the public good but commonly enough from the exigencies of politics and the attractions of revenue-raising.

The opportunity for taxing publications had helped in abolishing censorship at the end of the seventeenth century, when the advantage over outright prohibition was realised. Hence some improvements long predated the key years, 1830–1850, whereas others lagged until far later. The Court of Chancery slumbered on, recruitment to the civil service was only slowly secured by competitive examination (even then favouring public schoolboys and Oxbridge graduates), and commissions in the armed forces were being sold as late as 1871. By that time reform had fortunately moved a good way forwards, advanced by a roll-call of giant figures. William Cobbett had railed against the 'Old Corruption', meaning the sweets and sinecures handed out as rewards by the government; he and 'Orator' Hunt mobilised against it. From 1820 to 1823 John Wade documented the abuses in *The Black Book, or Corruption Unmasked*. The Combination Acts that had rendered trade union action illegal were repealed in 1824 and 1825. The death penalty was abolished for one hundred crimes and in 1829 Peel established a police force (the 'Peelers'). The Municipal Corporations Act was passed in 1834, vesting powers for improvement in town government instead of relying on ad hoc commissioners to arrange paving and cleansing. Elections to local government were established and a rate could now be levied. The Tithe Commutation Act soon followed, with its practical advantages for farmers, while factories and mines became better regulated.

Among the forces that combined to clean up the country, the voice of the Evangelicals was important; their zeal relegated the lifestyle of the Regency Bucks to dark corners. Bentham's influence, too, was profound and pragmatism like his was put into practice by that greatest of reformers, Edwin Chadwick, although only when Nassau Senior had helped to secure Chadwick's role. Chadwick was indefatigable in writing reports, instrumental in reforming the poor law, and endlessly effective in improving urban sanitation via the Public Health Act of 1848. His effectiveness would have been greater or come sooner without the attempts to exclude him from the most influential roles on the grounds that he lacked a sufficiently elevated background. Social snobbery worked against rational employment practices but Chadwick persevered. 'His achievements live on in every home and in every street in Britain', was one well-deserved encomium.

The New Poor Law of 1834 regularised unemployment and old-age provision, although the medicine was bitter. The indigent had been left to themselves in the draughty, tumbledown village poor houses but the workhouses which replaced them were no more than 'penal settlements for the elderly'. The Unions or 'grubbers' were meant to be feared, just as Lord Bathurst, Secretary of State for the Colonies, intended transportation to be feared. Later generations were marginally less severe on the aged poor. Chartism and the Anti-Corn Law League emerged after the '1830s in response to disappointment that reform had not immediately delivered everything radicals and the working populace wished.

Even then it was Australia rather than England that satisfied most of the Chartists' demands.[5] But Chartism's spectre did arouse the thought or fear of reform among English vested interests. Chartism and the Anti-Corn Law League, the latter fronted by Richard Cobden and John Bright, combined with the exertions of other reformers and government commissions, were needed to revive the hopes of the early 1830s.

After the Whigs had failed to secure the national finances during William IV's reign, Peel succeeded in introducing an income tax in 1842. It relieved the weight of indirect taxation that had held down spending on manufactures and so helped the home market to expand. Although much remained to be done—Asa Briggs thought Parliament could have been more completely reformed—the struggles of the 1830s and 1840s advanced a fair distance towards the superior public provision and orderliness of Victorian England. Curiously, the effect was best embodied overseas: 'Marvellous Melbourne' was the one city outside England to feature in Briggs's *Victorian Cities*. It showed what urban planning could do on a canvas free from the English legacy of irregular layouts and implacable interests. The connoisseur can see the effects of rationality even more clearly in the regular plan of Sale, Victoria, a small town not yet swamped, as Melbourne has been, by modern expansion.

Peel's central change was the Repeal of the Corn Laws in 1846–1849, which expanded the market for other goods by reducing the price of a loaf of bread. A head of pressure for this had been built up by the remarkable organisation of the Anti-Corn Law League.[6] Peel listened and Parliament eventually enacted Repeal, a free trade measure that struck the landed interest a serious but delayed blow. Arable England was buoyed up for one more generation through the natural protection afforded by too small an overseas supply of grain to call on, and by too little shipping capacity. But eventually Repeal was to sideline the cereal sector's 'Voice of Norfolk' in favour of livestock farmers, dairymen and the urban bourgeoisie in their northern industrial heartlands. Politics could now better reflect the needs of the manufacturing sector. Relatively speaking, Manchester rose and for the time being London fell.

Part of Victorian advance was the effect on working-class life. Back-to-back housing, stunted factory workers and deplorable conditions down the coal mines might make one sceptical of the benefits of industry. Industrialisation as such was no quick panacea, especially for the workers engaged in it. Sanitary reform and a cheaper loaf were a greater help in improving living standards, life expectancy and human energy.

Accordingly reform and regulation deserve credit for early improvement. Just as too much agricultural advance is taken to have been the result of the most prominent change, Parliamentary enclosure, so too much of the improvement in the quality of life is attributed directly to the factory. Contrary to Lord Kelvin's dictum that not being able to measure something means knowledge is meagre, it is because enclosures and factories are measurable—and hence measured to the exclusion of broader changes—that knowledge of the full processes of agrarian and industrial growth remains incomplete.

Notes

1. A. Bick, 'Bernard Mandeville and the "Economy" of the Dutch', *Erasmus Journal of Philosophy and Economics* I (1) (2008), p. 91.
2. E. L. Jones and M. E. Falkus, 'Urban Improvement and the English Economy in the Seventeenth and Eighteenth Centuries', *Research in Economic History* 4 (1979), pp. 193–233.
3. G. M. Trevelyan, *History of England* (London: Longmans, and Company, 1942 edition), p. 637; see also Geoffrey B. A. M. Finlayson, *England in the Eighteen Thirties* (London: Edward Arnold, 1969).
4. Asa Briggs, 'Reforming Acts', BBC website/archives, 17 Feb 2011.
5. Everything except annual parliaments, the one thing needed, it has been said, to keep parliamentarians honest.
6. Paul A. Pickering and Alex Tyrrell, *The People's Bread: A History of the Anti-Corn Law League* (London: Leicester University Press, 2000).

PART II

Coping with Shocks

CHAPTER 10

Disease

Diseases can be endemic or epidemic. Both act by decreasing the supply of labour, either through death or by reducing the work effort of enervated survivors who get sick but do not die. The effects differ according to the age groups most affected, whether towns are struck more than country, and so on. This indicates that even the worst shocks, such as the bubonic plague, were not truly exogenous since they did not fall on uniform populations, a fact which modified their effects. Plague's impact was concentrated in poor communities and over-crowded towns, where endemic disease also took its main toll. But societies and economies tend to adapt to the presence of endemic disease whereas the shocks of epidemics are abrupt and unpredictable, not only causing loss but capable of disturbing basic economic relationships like the ratio of labour to capital. A common opinion is that abnormal events put the normal working of societies into relief and are valuable social science experiments. With this in mind, writers pay special attention to the losses and upsets caused by epidemics, although in the long run endemic disease may have levied a higher toll on the economy.

Virtually no defences existed against epidemics, certainly not medical ones, and the toll was high. Because they did not have a linear history, they were in the eyes of the population unaccountable 'acts of God'. People were inclined to explain them in terms of their own moral failings, a self-defeating fatalism encouraged by the churches, whose finger continues to be pointed at whichever aspect of immorality it is fashionable to deplore. Medical science and theology being ineffective, the only sensible

E. L. Jones, *Barriers to Growth*, Palgrave Studies in Economic History,
https://doi.org/10.1007/978-3-030-44274-3_10

disasters may hit both factors of production at the same time. Thus the Black Death destroyed labour yet left capital untouched or at any rate re-usable, while technical knowledge also survived. This was 'growth by neutron bomb', with many people killed but capital and what the classical economists called capital-in-land going unscathed.[7] Recovery was possible because generous stretches of abandoned farmland now lay open for reoccupation by the survivors.

Achieving growth by this backhanded means was undeniably as cruel as it was inadvertent, yet in a long-term analytical sense it was effective. Except, that is, where it was not. The Western European response was not repeated in Eastern Europe. In principle, the decreased supply of labour should have produced comparable results there too but it failed to do so: a simple factor proportions argument will not hold. The great landowners of Eastern Europe were able to hold down the returns to scarce labour, sometimes even managing to re-feudalise their societies and make the peasants serfs again. In Western Europe, the landscape was more varied and the lords there had been unable to prevent labour from absconding or securing better terms. When attempts were made to re-impose serfdom in England they failed. The primary reason lay in a legal tradition which had become more autonomous and less a direct tool of the ruling classes. Eastern Europe benefited from no such tradition.

After the Plague of 1666, the next dramatic disease was smallpox, dramatic chiefly because of the way it was eventually contained. During the seventeenth century, smallpox had occurred in London as epidemics, each followed the year after by outbreaks elsewhere in the country. The stories about Lady Mary Wortley Montagu and inoculation and about Edward Jenner and vaccination are deservedly well known. As to measles, fatal but lesser outbreaks recurred in the eighteenth century. Prevalent diphtheria and scarlet fever were attributed by Howe to domestic overcrowding, which also encouraged the spread of typhus communicated by lice. Howe calls summer diarrhoea a fly-borne disease prevalent because of ubiquitous animal manure. The insanitary character of much of the country until the last decades of the twentieth century would be a surprise to current generations unused to swarms of insects, including flies.

Howe specialised in environmental aspects of medical geography an was among the first to chart now-familiar aspects of disease distributio such as that in relatively recent times all places with very high mort ity rates, apart from three London boroughs, were northern and west industrial cities.[8] He characterised medieval dwellings as dark, vermin

The reduction in malaria's incidence arose from causes that were multi-factorial. They were not the outcome of specific inventions or policies but stemmed from developments in unrelated areas. These can best be seen as the beneficial outcomes of a subtle rise in living standards not directly attributable to any single invention of the type usually thought responsible for economic growth. Broad-front and unintended consequences therefore presaged and accompanied the appearance of what is customarily thought of as the industrial revolution. Beyond this gradualism, and rather later, it was the public health officer enforcing state regulation who was more responsible than the doctor for eliminating the bulk of prominent killers. Local authorities had already fought the contagion of smallpox by isolating sufferers in the little 'pest houses' still to be found just outside some settlements. There is no doubt that disease had hampered economic activity and that the enabling conditions were largely environmental, just as were some of the remedies. Growth had not been stifled by disease but full resource mobilisation and therefore maximum economic efficiency was impaired. Society, fumbling towards solutions for disease problems, found one scourge replaced by another. England put one foot forward but set itself back on the other because starkly unequal incomes led to the overcrowding and poverty that were conducive to TB.

Notes

1. Quoted by E. L. Jones in Seventh International Economic History Congress, Edinburgh 1978, Four 'A' Themes, p. 26.
2. Eric L. Jones, 'Disaster Management and Resource Saving in Europe, 1400–1800', in Antoni Maczak and William N. Parker (eds.), *Natural Resources in European History* (Washington, DC: Resources for the Future, 1978), pp. 114–136.
3. James Chambers, *The English House* (New York: W. W. Norton, 1985), p. 187.
4. Wilfred Bonser, *The Medical Background of Anglo-Saxon England* (London: The Wellcome Historical Medical Library, 1968).
5. G. M. Howe, *Man, Environment and Disease in Britain* (New York: Barnes & Noble, 1972).
6. Bruce Campbell, *The Great Transition: Climate, Disease and Society in the Late-Medieval World* (Cambridge: Cambridge University Press, 2016).
7. J. L. Anderson and E. L. Jones, 'Natural Disasters and the Historical Response', *Ahustralian Economic History Review* XXVIII (1) (1988), p. 7.

8. G. Melvyn Howe, 'The Environment, Its Influence and Hazards to Health', in G. Melvyn Howe and John A. Lorraine (eds.), *Environmental Medicine* (London: Heinemann Medical Books, 1980 [1973]), pp. 1–7.
9. Among a number of papers on the historical distribution, prevalence and decline of malaria, see for example S. P. James, 'The Disappearance of Malaria from England', *Proceedings* of the Royal Society of Medicine 23 (1) (1929), pp. 71–87, especially for the dramatic graph of declining incidence, 1847–1922, and Mary Dobson, '"Marsh Fever"—The Geography of Malaria in England', *Journal of Historical Geography* 6 (4) (1980), pp. 357–389.

CHAPTER 11

Insults to Agriculture

Animal diseases may be divided into two, like their human equivalents, on the one hand, endemic and on the other epidemic or rather epizootic. These categories by no means exhaust the 'insults' to which agriculture was subject, which included, as they still do, plant diseases, weeds and predation by birds and animals, and weather events which we will deal with separately. Nor do they fully distinguish between sudden onslaughts that are best termed shocks—seldom heralded and hard to deal with even when there was a little warning—and more gradual assaults such as competing organisms always pruning the crops. To judge from the way they are ignored, many of these problems strike historians and economists as obscure and trivial. Yet the cost could be significant and the immediate effects were a constant complaint in the writings of farmers. The burden was heavy when agriculture constituted so much more of the economy than it does today. Huge numbers of works exist about the various problems of agriculture, gathering force from the mid-seventeenth century. This literature is alternately dogmatic and baffled as the insults were faced and a means desperately sought to cope with the consequences.

Compared with problems besetting industry or mining, the biological troubles affecting agriculture were intractable and prone constantly to recur. Relevant science developed very slowly. Despite efforts that were collated by Hartlib in Cromwellian times, boosted by the Royal Society from 1660 and canvassed by forward-looking provincial bodies, effective remedies remained few.[1] Modes of dealing with agricultural risk could be elaborate, involving managerial moves, even contortions, in all types of

E. L. Jones, *Barriers to Growth*, Palgrave Studies in Economic History,
https://doi.org/10.1007/978-3-030-44274-3_11

husbandry.[2] In England veterinary science developed at a glacial pace.[3] Veterinary schools opened a generation later than on the continent, the first not being established until 1791. Practitioners lacked social status and possessed too little influence. It was the more prominent Royal Society of Agriculture which persuaded the government to adopt a policy of slaughter in the rinderpest outbreak of 1865 but even after that there was no significant public expenditure on research into livestock diseases until the twentieth century. Epizootics were thought of as imported problems, to be controlled by restrictive legislation as they occurred—the 'stamping out' method. A formal investigation of the immensely severe outbreak of liver rot in sheep during the wet seasons of 1879 to 1880 could still come up with only 'rather general recommendations'.[4] Suggested measures continued to be in the realm of husbandry management rather than biology, as they always had been and sometimes continue to be.

Agriculture aims to divert energy from plants and animals to human uses and the process offers many targets to competing species. The further the move from subsistence to commerce, the more crops were sown as monocultures and the larger became flocks and herds, increasingly of single breeds. This presented concentrated sources of food for opportunistic species and renewed the vulnerability every season. Pests which utilised human activities and food sources throve under this regime; measures against them were feeble, expensive in terms of foregone opportunities, and seldom completely successful. They represented an impediment to economic growth that by its nature neither could nor ever can be wholly overthrown. The chronic uncertainty faced by early farmers isolated in their small communities bred superstition, just as uncertainty about all human affairs encouraged belief in spells and pseudo-sciences like astrology. Remedies were displacement activities which targeted some coincidentally occurring organism or practice and were repeated uncritically for lack of alternatives, as when Suffolk farmers maintained that to cut thistles before St. John's Day (24 June) meant that two would grow where only one grew before. The church became involved and even in Protestant countries met the challenge by 'excommunicating' pests. Prayers to the gods of ancient times were mimicked by the church. This practice has never entirely ceased: clergy can still be found claiming that pestilence and crop failure, like human disease, are celestial punishments for sin. Imperfect observation, restricted markets, a lack of science, the credulity of the under-educated, and the self-interest of the clergy ensured this 'survival of the mediocre'.[5]

Anything that might conceivably work was tried. Despite their dangers, arsenical and copper-based seed steeps to prevent crop disease were popular during the eighteenth- and nineteenth centuries. Innumerable other substances were applied to control pests, some of the purported remedies tending to overkill.[6] In principle, substances could be tested but double-blind tests were seldom carried out. For managerial solutions there was no universal market to impose its own tests. Comparatively little existed by way of arrangements to diffuse knowledge or compare effects beyond the locality or at most the county. Agricultural societies offered non-pecuniary rewards such as rosettes or cups presented at annual shows. The approach suffered from the 'prize marrow fallacy', rewarding success by giving awards for the largest or heaviest products rather than the most profitable. This pandered to vanity, although useful outcomes did sometimes put in an appearance, as with selectively bred fat stock. The auction ring provided a limited market test where animals could be bought or hired out at stud to spread improved strains but it was geographically segmented, as the proliferation of regional breeds suggests. Crops had less exposure to market tests than livestock; what they were exposed to was less tractable—diseases or pest species that found ceaseless opportunities in the fields.

Among the most devastating problems faced by farmers was liver rot in sheep.[7] Wet and passably warm summers provide favourable conditions for infestation with parasitic liver flukes, *Fasciola hepatica*, for which the sole vector is a tiny water snail, *Lymnaea truncatula*. Like many snails, this species aestivates (the summer equivalent of hibernation) in dry years. When there are four or more consecutive summer months during which rainfall exceeds evaporation, the population of this snail may explode. Sheep ingest the snails and with them the liver fluke, which brings the rot and leads to high mortality among the flocks.

Rainfall persistent enough to foment outbreaks occurs every six or seven years in the wetter, warmer half of the country and at longer intervals nationwide.[8] Even when sheep do not die in large numbers, they 'go back' in condition, and despite sales of diseased animals the financial loss can range from merely heavy to exorbitant. This is true even when we allow for two complicating factors. One is the profit made by sharp operators who trade in diseased sheep, which fatten faster than healthy animals. Robert Bakewell, the eighteenth-century livestock breeder and one of the so-called fathers of the agricultural revolution, regularly flooded his pastures to induce the rot in sheep meant for the butcher, thereby gaining five or six weeks over his neighbours. The other factor is the exaggeration inherent in the way whereby the agricultural community tends to estimate its financial losses, which is by physical loss multiplied by a target price without allowing for alterations in prices when supply or demand change. Nevertheless, there were years when the monetary cost for many producers must have been immense, given the sheer scale of the loss of animals. The two largest outbreaks were from 1828 to 1831, when a loss of two million sheep was claimed, and 1879 to 1881 when six million died or had to be slaughtered.

Farmers well knew that the clay vales were worse hit by liver rot than the drier uplands. The two types of land can be close together, so close that they may coexist on individual farms straddling the escarpments between vale and downland. The comparatively few farmers in those situations did gain some understanding but it did not extend to a veterinary cure, only to manoeuvres to limit the exposure of their flocks. Exponents of enclosure had their say, arguing that the commons were not drained and this conduced to the rot. The poor man's sheep rotted and everyone's animals mingled with them anyhow, permitting other diseases to spread unchecked. Agricultural improvement brought a limited remedy by extending drainage on the clays, but seldom until the end of the eighteenth century and not significantly until the third quarter of the nineteenth century.

Whereas the rot grumbled away on the least-drained farms in many seasons, the cattle plague struck at long intervals but was devastating when it came. Rinderpest, also known as Steppe Murrain, had come from abroad, appearing in England only from 1709 to 1720 and during some later phases of the eighteenth century. Losses in certain localities were high enough to elicit practical sympathy and permission was granted to send round 'briefs' of the type ordinarily used to solicit charitable donations after town fires. As an example, money was raised in 1715 and 1716 'for the Cowkeepers of Middlesex', whose dense herds may have been particularly hard hit.[9] Laws to regulate the cattle trade came later. From December 1749, all long-distance movement of beasts was banned for three months, but the edict was so speedily repealed it had no effect. An Order in Council of 1768 may have been more useful through banning the import of hides, hoofs and the horns of cattle from parts of north-western Europe where violent 'distemper' was raging.[10] Forbidding movements of livestock and shutting the countryside down, which even today is the response to foot-and-mouth outbreaks, was far from costless, since it involved putting up physical barriers against the introduction of the disease to farms, closing markets and paying compensation for animals slaughtered because they were infected or had been in contact with sick animals. Compensated slaughter was introduced again during the Rinderpest outbreak of 1865.

Turning to pests of larger dimensions than disease organisms, a wide array of birds, mammals and insects are all capable of surging in numbers to prey on crops. Casual observations were often over-extended and harmless species grouped among the targets for control. From the sixteenth century, parishes were empowered to pay bounties for the heads or tails of a wide range of species and did so almost everywhere, especially for house sparrows, but including utterly innocuous birds. Among definite pests, fecund rabbits and flocking species such as wood pigeons and rooks can all eat the fields bare; farmers are loath to admit that this may be offset by plants growing again later in the season or birds feeding on insects as well as seeds.

Insect pests attracted special attention but only gradually elicited a scientific response. Many of the earliest entomologists were moneyed men who were dilettante, an exception being John Curtis (1791–1862), who made his way, turning from writing popular books to becoming an economic entomologist hired by the Royal Agricultural Society.[11] His advice was sensible but no silver bullet was found. Instead what were little more than folk remedies were applied: schoolchildren were paid to collect huge numbers of cabbage white butterflies whose caterpillars can devastate brassica crops, something that was considered urgent at times of national food shortage such as the First World War.

Century after century, farmers were embroiled in struggles to protect their crops from pests and afterwards to keep stored grain safe from rats and mice by raising their granaries on little pillars called staddle stones. Some of the problems were overblown whereas others were all too real. Few were open to permanent solutions. The temptation to sow dense monocultures and the consequent raids by pests guaranteed an annual round of damage. Killing pests by any available means never succeeded in eliminating them, merely thinned them out. This amounted to 'rat farming', whereby the pests which did survive had the choice of the best breeding sites and best food supplies, enabling their numbers to multiply fast for the next round of onslaughts. A parallel issue was weeds, which were also recurrent and resistant to conclusive elimination. If we consider the manifold insults to agriculture in the broad and long, we can see they were an unending burden which were rarely lifted to satisfaction. Despite ceaseless effort and expense, pests were reduced but seldom decisively vanquished, most definitely not before or during the time of the industrial revolution. Unlike some other sectors of the economy, and despite its obvious importance, the agricultural sector was almost permanently hampered because pests and diseases continually recruited themselves. What could not be cured had to be endured.

Notes

1. The Bath & West Society set up a Committee of Chemical Research and a laboratory as early as 1805, the first organised by a provincial agricultural society. A medical doctor was appointed to analyse the region's soils as the first 'Chemical Professor to the Society.' David Jeremy, *Henry Wansey and His American Journal* (Philadelphia: American Philosophical Society, 1970), p. 18.
2. A most comprehensive study of ecological management deals with the marginal environment of the Swiss Alps. Dodgshon, *Farming Communities in the Western Alps.*
3. D. H. M. Fraser, *Veterinary Science and the Colonial Administration in the Machakas and Kitui Districts of Kenya, 1895–1938* (Cambridge Master's thesis, 2010, seen by courtesy of Mr. Owen Humphreys).
4. Abigail Woods, 'From Conducted Campaigns to Watertight Compartments: Diseased Sheep and Their Investigation in Britain, c.1880–1920', in Abigail Woods et al., *Animals and the Shaping of Modern Medicine* (Basingstoke: Palgrave Macmillan, 2018), p. 72.
5. For modern examples included in a compendium of historical beliefs and practices, see D. M. Secoy and A. E. Smith, 'Superstition and Social Practices Against Agricultural Pests', *Environmental Review* 5 (1978), pp. 2–18.
6. Allan E. Smith and Diane M. Secoy, 'A Compendium of Inorganic Substances Used in European Pest Control Before 1850', *Agricultural and Food Chemistry* 24 (6) (1976), pp. 1180–1186; M. Holmes, 'Melancholy Consequences: Britain's Long Relationship with Agricultural Chemistry Since the Mid-Eighteenth Century', *Environment and History* 25 (1) (2019), pp. 117–120.
7. E. L. Jones, *Seasons and Prices: The Role of the Weather in English Agricultural History* (London: Allen & Unwin, 1964).
8. Current or recent rainfall is not a foolproof predictor of flooding. The lavants of which Gilbert White wrote, and the bournes of the chalklands as a whole, rise and may flood with a lag of some months.

9. Rev. Canon Oldfield, 'Church Briefs', *Berks, Bucks and Oxon Archaeological Journal* XVIII (1913), p. 50.
10. *Annual Register*, 9 Aug 1768, p. 153.
11. George Ordish, *John Curtis and the Pioneering of Pest Control* (Reading: Osprey, 1974).

CHAPTER 12

Storms and Adverse Seasons

Only a tiny proportion of historical writing deals with the effects of natural phenomena, concentrating instead on political or social processes, with the natural world figuring, if at all, as a mere backcloth. In certain strands of Marxism, no independent influence of factors outside society is countenanced. At the opposite extreme are those writers, commonly natural scientists, who are constantly searching for universal keys to history in some external force and representing humanity as its pawn. Writers of this temperament once thought they had found what they were looking for in celestial interventions, ad hoc punishments from above. In a more secular age they believe, with the power of an idee fixe, that they have come across the answer in fluctuations of the climate. Historically there was seldom a fully persuasive correlation.[1]

During the fifteenth century, the cultivated area contracted more or less in time with the deterioration from warmth in the Middle Ages to the early modern Little Ice Age. But the causality is suspect because the trend of agricultural prices was downwards, not upwards, showing that it was not a climatic constraint which was restricting cultivation. Instead, arable land was being put down to pasture or tumbling down to waste because of a fall in demand. Decreasing quantities of grain were needed to feed a population that was repeatedly pruned by recurrences of the plague during the century after the Black Death. Samuel Rudder, writing in 1779 and cited previously, may not have picked the right motive for explaining the outcome but he was correct in indicting human agency (responses to

E. L. Jones, *Barriers to Growth*, Palgrave Studies in Economic History,
https://doi.org/10.1007/978-3-030-44274-3_12

the plague) rather than climate change. Natural events and trends should not be ignored but they are filtered through society's ability to adapt.

England's unstable weather systems did subject the country to repeated buffeting. Storms did enormous damage. The eustatic movement that is slowly tilting south-eastern England under the sea renders that region especially vulnerable. This highlights the at-risk or what (extending the usage) we may label the 'demand' side of disasters alongside the 'supply' of severe weather; the two combined produce the worst harm. Thus the thirteenth and fourteenth centuries witnessed storms that caused Dunwich on the Suffolk coast to be abandoned, despite having been the tenth-largest town in the country in the eleventh century. Ironically, England's habit of retaining institutions when their purpose is long past meant that Dunwich held onto the right to send two MPs to Westminster until the Reform Act of 1832!

Moving to periods with which we are more concerned, 'the greatest storm', one of the most extreme ever, lasted for several days at the end of November 1703.[2] It was famously described by Daniel Defoe. Much shipping was sunk, hundreds of windmills were damaged or destroyed, and the small town of Loddon, Norfolk, was said to have burned down—although no mention of this appears in any of the several websites about the town's history. The author of *An Exact Relation of the Late Dreadful Tempest*, published in 1704 in the immediate aftermath of the storm, recorded a large number of instances of damage by wind and flood but followed the habit of his times in treating the event as a punishment by God. Obviously for a trading nation, the loss of shipping was serious nor can exceptionally widespread damage on land be doubted. But observations made in the heat of the moment, if that is not an inappropriate metaphor, were too anecdotal to permit calculating the total cost and several modern studies have been more interested in the meteorological aspects. One retrospective is however inclined to think the storm a genuine national calamity.[3] This source collects reports of physical damage, makes the remarkable claim that a majority of houses in Southern Britain were partly or wholly stripped of their tiles, and computes the loss at six million pounds. Precisely how contemporary assertions about physical losses were translated into monetary costs does not appear.

A similar limitation in approach applies to the collection of inadequately documented reports in T. H. Baker's *Record of Seasons, Prices and Phenomena* (1883), although it does include claims that in 1703 London sustained two million pounds worth of damage; eight thousand people lost their lives in floods along the Severn, the Thames and the coast of Holland; fifteen thousand sheep were drowned in one (unnamed) place; and a remarkably precise 1107 houses and barns were destroyed in Kent.[4] According to Baker wheat was twice the 1703 price by the spring of 1704. Brayne's modern account, which cites a large number of contemporary diaries, can do little better by way of adding up the overall cost and its figures for wider losses are unpersuasive.[5] Despite the inexactitude, the total harm was considerable, although not large enough to rank among the string of national calamities famously enumerated by Adam Smith.

Storms were frequent over the years and sometimes had interesting consequences. One in 1710 destroyed the roof of a church at Greenwich, just when the erection of St. Paul's Cathedral after London's Great Fire of 1666 was at last nearing completion. Parliament diverted the coal tax levied to pay for St Paul's to rebuild the Greenwich church as one of 50 proposed new churches. In the event, only eleven of these 'Queen Anne Churches' were actually built but with important architectural consequences.[6] Another storm of interest occurred at Lyme Regis, Dorset, in November 1824, when the tide destroyed several houses, a hotel and four ships. It washed from one of the houses a longcase clock, constructed about 1760, which was later found and is now in the town museum. From our distance in time such events, frequent enough and in this case known as Lyme's 'Great Storm', nevertheless amounted to only a local tragedy.[7]

Little could be done in the short run to guard against storm damage, but we should note that shipping was made safer by the provision of lighthouses. They began to appear during the early eighteenth century and were at first private initiatives, recouping the investment by a legal right to levy a charge on vessels passing by or using some nearby harbour. The Eddystone Light, first erected in the 1690s, was actually demolished by the 'greatest storm' of 1703, though fairly soon replaced. On land, storm danger could not be signalled decisively in the way lighthouses could warn of rocks, besides which capital losses took some time to restore. In the aftermath of 1703, roofs in Somerset had to be replaced with reed thatch instead of tile, for lack of alternative. In the long run, better building materials did offer some protection, although this did not extend to the poor for whom there may anyhow have been little sympathy: the vicar of Fairford, Gloucestershire, proclaimed that to dwell on the fate of poor cottagers, 'would be frivolous as well as vexatious'.[8]

With respect to other problems with the weather—persistent rain, low temperatures, snowy winters or drought—two different types of remedy existed or came into being. One was the indirect result of economic growth itself, such as houses made of sturdier materials, more suitable choices of sites for production, and improved distributions of farming and land use. The advance of the brick frontier amounted to a weather-proofing of houses (initially those of the well-to-do) with brick walls and tile roofs. Besides announcing one's status, the main purpose was to minimise fire risk but one side effect was healthier dwellings and another was greater resilience in times of bad weather. The other type of remedy comprised specific inventions meant to mitigate the effects of adverse weather, but such devices tended to be minor and appeared rather late in Victorian times. The most significant was the Dutch barn with a fixed roof which was introduced from the 1880s. It was probably as useful in saving the labour of thatching the ricks as in keeping out the wet.

Changes in agricultural distributions not only secured food supplies against bad weather but had the related effect of smoothing out seasonality. The advances were regionally patterned since crops and rotations are seldom suitable for all locations and soil types. An example was the system of floated water meadows that colonised the valley bottoms of Southern England during the seventeenth- and eighteenth centuries. They were expressly designed to grow feed for filling the 'hungry gap' between winter and spring, when the previous year's stock of fodder was running out and new growth had not yet sprung. Water meadows encouraged an early bite of grass and made it possible to carry flocks of sheep through the 'cruellest month' of April and to facilitate early lambing. Less often acknowledged is the regional effect of the next tier of innovations, the sowing of clover, turnips and 'artificial' grasses, although we mentioned this somewhat neglected change in crop-growing when discussing both enclosure and tithes. Besides supplementing animal feed, these fodder crops made it possible to over-winter sheep and cattle on the wolds and downs, softening the worst seasons on cold, high ground, reducing the flows of livestock needing to be agisted in the vales and depressing the price of water meadow, which therefore lost its monopoly of providing extra feed in the worst spring gap. Dry seasons could still oblige hill farmers to drive their beasts down for agistment in the more sheltered valleys but not to the former extent.

Further innovations in cropping also increased resilience. Common turnips were susceptible to frost, which threatened to leave animals short of feed in winter. One response was the introduction of swedes, or Swedish turnips, from the end of the eighteenth century. They were hard but could be chopped into bite-sized pieces that even a toothless old ewe could eat. Swedes were thus a supplement to winter feed in the turnip-growing, sheep-rearing districts and we have seen that their introduction was a bone of contention between enterprising farmers and the tithe owners. A comparable advance which came rather later, in the mid-nineteenth century, took the form of introducing another hardy root crop, this time on the clays: mangel-wurzel.

Changed agricultural distributions could have wide application. By enabling production to be relocated to more suitable districts they could subtly combat the worst seasonality. Severe winters, long droughts and sizeable floods might affect broad acreages, though seldom enough to have a truly national impact. Nor were the effects always long-lasting, taking that to mean for more than one harvest year. The most striking events tended to be local and probably short-term; furthermore, given the intricate patterns of English geology, topography and ecology, they had a habit of cancelling out. Losses in one area might be made up by gains in another, not always far distant, where the weather had struck less violently. And the failure of one product might be offset by good receipts from another. Any number of striking incidents may be strung together in narrative accounts, yet there is no certainty they depressed the economy as a whole. Parish-level records do not aggregate readily and their implications are not easily fathomed given the differences between dramatic and merely uncomfortable experiences and between physical destruction and economic cost.

Consider the problem of hailstorms which are often thought to be particularly harmful, a recorded example being one that hit four parishes in the Kennet Valley, Berkshire, in 1762.[9] It did a great deal of damage, with seven hundred acres of crops laid waste, losses assessed at £1143, and a brief issued to ask for charitable contributions. Hailstorms can be devastating when they hit like this and it is not surprising that hail was an early subject for insurance, superseding the informal risk-sharing offered by briefs, although not until 1842. For unlucky people, hail storms could be tragic but their wider significance was quite limited.

Less concentrated problems included long, cold, snowy winters; and drought and the opposite, persistent rain. Any of these could affect great swathes of the country but more often they affected a few districts. Little could be done to guard against cold and snow or (before field pumps) drought, which in the drier eastern half of the country has always been more significant than stereotypes of a wet English climate might lead one to assume. Rain was more general and could impede a number of tasks, the chief being the mowing, carrying and storing of the hay crop. Relative to the harvest of grain, the hay harvest was more critical than may appear, since the suitable window of time for it is narrow and livestock depend on it. This faced farmers with a capacity problem, since when the opportunity of haying presented itself they needed extra hands quickly but only temporarily. Labour shortages were sometimes met by drafting women in for mowing, in addition to their more ordinary task of following the mowers and gathering the crop. Apart from managerial manoeuvres of that type, little could be done apart from making sure the stacks were tightly thatched.

Great tracts of England were very damp, at least in some years and certain seasons. Just how damp is shown by the land-making and water engineering carried out in estate after estate by 'Capability' Brown and other eighteenth-century landscape gardeners. These men found straggling rivers and streams that were prone to overflow, and made it their business to tidy them into regular channels, creating a great many park lakes in the process. In rainy spells during the twenty-first century, streams still rise unexpectedly in many fields but there are now enough ditches for much of the water to drain away within a few days. In past centuries field drainage was poor to non-existent and nothing so mundane was tackled by the landscape gardeners; they were paid to attend to the aesthetics of scenery and prettify the estates of the rich. By contrast, farmland was often left very poorly drained, as may be seen from field names on the tithe maps of the 1830s, with parks among it like tame islands in a rough sea.

Farming remained much at the mercy of all the elements. Wet and windy summers might lodge the grain crops, that knocks them over and make them hard to reap. Wet autumns could saturate the soils and make it difficult or impossible to sow next year's crop. This was not visually dramatic and escaped the laments frequent in the valleys, especially the Severn and Avon where there were many excited remarks about haycocks floating downriver. Long spells of downpour gave some warning but there was only so much that could be done. Major drainage works that tackled the problem of floods, in the sense of continuous overflows caused by intense storms or persistent rain, are described in the next chapter. The routine experience of land made too wet to work by above-average rainfall could be tackled only by resolute field drainage. This was a matter of stone drains and burying lines of bushes through which water could percolate; neither was very effective or easy to maintain.

Clay tile drains were introduced at the end of the eighteenth century but only after 1845 were they mass-produced. During the third quarter of the nineteenth century, taxpayers' money was abundantly lent for field drainage, though estimates of the area concerned vary enormously. Contemporary estimates are unreliable and scholars despair: one suggests working through estate papers (which when they refer to the matter survive in only a minority of cases and would require decades of research), while another recommends a field-by-field search for surviving Victorian drains (which would be impossibly expensive and produce scanty results).[10] Suffice it to say that the land drained was extensive, especially in the north and west of the country, but no complete national coverage was achieved.[11] Under-drainage could be effective but its limitations should be recognised. The pertinent issue is not how extensively the stiff clays were drained but whether it was sufficient for them to compete in crop-growing with the light-soiled uplands, where natural drainage freed the equivalent investment for other purposes.

Viewed through the lens of the farming press, difficulties caused by the weather seem severe, as at times they definitely are on individual farms, in some places and over certain regions of the country. Maximum potential output was almost never achieved, which means that bad weather for someone, somewhere, was always posing a challenge and causing loss. It was a burden that could never be abolished but could eventually be minimised, once engines became available to speed up farm operations—long after the period of concern here. In any case, the way the weather varied from time to time and place to place, besides the speed with which it changed, made many effects cancel out.

Notes

1. J. L. Anderson and E. L. Jones, 'Natural Disasters and the Historical Response', *Australian Economic History Review* XXVIII/1 (1988), pp. 3–20.
2. Martin Brayne, *The Greatest Storm* (Stroud: Sutton, 2002).
3. Risk Management Models, *December 1703 Windstorm: 300-Year Retrospective* (Risk Management Solutions, 2003), pp. 1–6.
4. T. H. Baker, *Records of the Seasons, Prices of Agricultural Produce, and Phenomena Observed in the British Isles* (London: Simpkin, Marshall, 1883), pp. 174–175.
5. Recent studies have attempted to put order into the vast number of contemporary references to the weather, usually atypical events, and mainly

found in parish registers. The large volume of material does not mean, however, that there is enough to provide a balanced and comprehensive record. The research is typically well-funded team work, collects much information and includes the digitization of sources, but has not so far produced usable generalisations about the economic effects of the weather. See e.g. Lucy Vale et al., '"Instead of Fetching Flowers, the Youths Brought in Flakes of Snow": Exploring Extreme Weather History Through English Parish Registers', *The Journal of the Archives and Records Association* 38 (1) (2017), pp. 119–142.

6. John Goodall, *Parish Church Treasures* (London: Bloomsbury Continuum, 2015), p. 185.
7. Thea Hawksworth, 'Great Storm Clock', Lyme Regis Museum *Paper no. 9*, 2016.
8. Quoted by Brayne, *Greatest Storm* (2002), p. 4.
9. E. L. Jones, *Seasons and Prices: The Role of the Weather in English Agricultural History* (London: Allen & Unwin, 1964), p. 38.
10. Finds of tile drains by the Severn in places where under-drainage took place after 1850 are described in John R. L. Allen, 'A Short History of Salt-Marsh Reclamation at Slimbridge Warth and Neighbouring Areas, Gloucestershire', *Transactions* of the Bristol and Gloucestershire Archaeological Society 104 (1986), pp. 139–155.
11. Nigel Harvey, *The Industrial Archaeology of Farming in England and Wales* (London: Batsford, 1980), pp. 82, 202. Harvey cites a calculation that 12 million acres were drained by the 1890s. This mostly dated before 1880 and is four times greater than contemporary estimates. In the 1970s the Ministry of Agriculture stated that the national cultivated area was 23 million acres, which (with all allowances for the different period) must make the estimate of 12 million acres drained improbable.

CHAPTER 13

Floods

Flooding took different forms in different times and places, and while the associated history of drainage may occasionally be traced in detail it too often remains obscure. The present chapter seeks to discern the trends in flooding and drainage inherent in what is a mixed bag of studies. Much is achievable but an exact figure for the proportion of the country where the fields were under-drained defeats the researcher and the area 'inned' from the sea or drained in the river basins is more uncertain still. Little would be added to understanding the issues by counting acreages, were it possible to obtain totals when few accounts are specific. Some coastal reclamation of medieval times was lost to later marine flooding and the activity of that period seems to have reached a crescendo before the Black Death only to tail off afterwards.[1] The bigger drainage schemes from Elizabeth's reign onwards are better known, with some, though not all, being the subject of numerous local studies. The usual purpose of drainage was the joint product of creating more cropland and preventing floods, with private gains for the investors from acquiring a share of marshland hitherto held in common and exploited for its natural resources. On some coastal marshes another purpose was to acquire land for grazing, at any rate during the summer, thereby freeing other parts of the estates for cropping. Seasonal inundation was acceptable on these pastures and they needed less expenditure on sea banks than would have been required to protect plough-land.

This is not to hint that flood control was merely contingent. Far from it when even reclaimed land continued to be at risk. We leave aside the

E. L. Jones, *Barriers to Growth*, Palgrave Studies in Economic History,
https://doi.org/10.1007/978-3-030-44274-3_13

records of medieval flooding and start with the flood along the Trent in 1600, which caused the river so to alter course that the village of Holme ended up on the opposite bank from where it had started.[2] Shortly afterwards, in 1607, intense flooding affected the North Somerset Levels and along the Severn in Gloucestershire, with thousands of livestock claimed as lost, while in the latter county bridges over tributaries of the main rivers were destroyed.[3] At Worcester are flood markers recording heights on the Severn at intervals over centuries; there, at any rate, it should have been hard to forget the threat. Floods were frequent and distressing but usually limited or at most regional in impact, so much so that they are hard to isolate as a recognisable influence on the national economy. When modern scholars study the economic impact of historical floods they often find it impossible to advance beyond the assertions of contemporaries about 'thousands' of livestock swept away.

A disarming feature of local or regional disaster history is that it almost always concentrates on the 'supply side', describing dramatic events and listing (to the limited extent that the sources permit) the physical losses. Financial losses are commonly mysteries or the subjects of ex cathedra pronouncements. Changes in what was at risk (the 'demand side' as opposed to the 'supply' of disasters like floods) are rarely discussed. This lopsided approach bedevils studies of much grander disasters, yet the implications are well known to the insurance markets. Modern studies draw attention to the way infrastructure and new housing continue to be permitted on flood-prone land. Occasionally they mention that far more capital is at risk than was previously the case and note that this can lead the unwary to think that losses are rising because of ever-worse flooding rather than that more structures are there to be affected. Increasing capital intensity is a feature of long-run history and the capital-to-labour loss ratio has altered. The value of the capital stock has risen but far fewer people are drowned in absolute, let alone relative, terms.

The ratio was different in the past, when the capital stock was smaller yet more people lived in agriculturally productive but vulnerable coastal or riverside situations without the benefit of organised rescue services and life-saving equipment. Some further differences may be noted. Far more of the hay crop once came from coastal marshes, river pastures and low-lying vales than is now the case. In the absence of transport that could move such a bulky commodity and with a heavy dependence on grass for feeding livestock, hay was disproportionately valuable to small semi-isolated farming communities. This began to change from the late

seventeenth- and again from the late eighteenth century, with the introduction and later intensified sowing of new fodder crops, permitting the relocation of much fodder production to the drier uplands. Accordingly, flood losses were likely to have dealt heftier blows to living standards the earlier we look.

It is needless to rehearse every example, every conflict with commoners, and every occasion when schemes failed or ceased to be maintained, only to be revived at later dates, notably, once steam pumps became available. A rapid survey of some major efforts, familiar and less familiar, will demonstrate that until recent centuries sizeable stretches of wetland across the country, especially in the Fens, were exploited more for their natural resources than for settled farming. They were brought into cultivation by fits and starts and the costs and benefits, though scarcely computable, deserve to be discussed. Moreover, the major projects fall into a surprising chronological pattern which also needs to be assessed.

The big projects designed to replace the pastoral commons' economy of the wetlands began at the end of the sixteenth century, if we leave aside those of the High Middle Ages and earlier times. Some of the endeavours were ancient and on a large scale. A graphic map prepared by Nigel Harvey shows successive extensions of the 'innings' that took in Romney Marsh from the twelfth to the seventeenth centuries.[4] Start, though, with the western side of England, where from 1630 to 1646 an over-ambitious attempt at draining the Fleet, on the landward side of Chesil Bank, Dorset, was a failure. Or with later success in the Upper Thames valley, where about 1800 a Grand Drain was constructed through Fairford and Kempsford, Gloucestershire. It was well-designed, with water wheels to lift one stream above another, and whereas the wheels have long vanished the Grand Drain continues to flow. One thousand acres were drained, with a further 300 acres covered by a supplementary Embankment Drain. We are left wondering how and by whom the enterprise was financed and how well it repaid the investors.

Rudge's *General View* of the agriculture of Gloucestershire, written about 1805, attributes the design to Edward Webb of Stow-on-the-Wold, a surveyor and civil engineer whose assistant, William Smith, became the discoverer of stratigraphy and 'father of geology'.[5] Hugh Torrens states that Smith himself engaged in a number of drainage projects.[6] He worked from 1802 to 1804 for the Lords Eliot, father and son, at Down Ampney, a few miles west of the Grand Drain, where the modern map and landscape show a geometric pattern of long ditches. An impressive tunnel carries an artificial cut under a track on the estate. Elsewhere along the Upper Thames projects on a par with the Grand Drain were not successfully undertaken until the 1850s and 1860s, when they were carried out a few miles upstream from Oxford. Even today the entire Upper Thames is an area of high flood risk. Many pastures display streams whose canalisation dates back for one, probably for two, thousand years but their effectiveness was incomplete and their maintenance fluctuated. Prior to the 1860s there was only unproductive rough grass in many areas and at times the land was so wet that mowers worked without shoes or stockings.[7]

None of the efforts along the Upper Thames has attracted attention. Book after book restricts discussion to the admittedly far grander exploits in the East Anglian Fens, to a lesser extent the Somerset Levels, and in a minority of publications to Romney Marsh. Progress is recorded, too, for such places as Canvey Island, Hatfield Chase, the Isle of Axholme, Martin Mere, the Lancashire Mosses, in the Lincolnshire Fens, along the Severn estuary and around the Solent, in all or most of which the intermittent progress of reclamation went back several centuries. One source concerning Canvey Island asks a question that is seldom explicitly raised: what was the chronology of reclaiming land from the marsh?[8] The answer at Canvey was from 1620 to 1625, with four smaller additions until 1770 and four more during the 1850s.

This periodicity in Canvey Island was not quite matched in other districts. The sizeable lake in Somerset called Meare Pool was reclaimed in stages after 1620, with new cuts made about 1660, two rivers canalised in the late 1730s, and the Pool gone from maps by the mid-eighteenth century. According to close scrutiny of evidence about land around the Solent, ninety per cent of the total marsh pasture was reclaimed in the phases 1600–1720, 1780–1820 and 1850–1890, a small remainder having been tackled before 1700 or even before 1600.[9] In this area, it was thought worth erecting sea-banks to stop the tide flooding the pastures. In the classic Fenland of Eastern England, five drainage schemes were revived after 1660, having been abandoned during the Civil War.[10] Two were failures; the other three proved successful, although the measure may simply be the lack of further resistance which had dragged on in some places. Griffiths' exemplary study of the fairly small drainage works on the coastal marshes of north Norfolk from 1633 to about 1643 also mentions revived activity during the late 1640s and early 1650s, and again from 1693 to 1720.[11] Even there the peak of activity dated from before the Civil War. How many other piecemeal efforts took place at any period can only be guessed; few sources stating actual costs and receipts like the Le Strange notebooks for Hunstanton, used by Griffiths, seem likely to surface.

The type specimen among schemes was the draining of the Great Level of the Fens in the early seventeenth century by Cornelius Vermuyden, and while his personal role has been downplayed by modern research, the overall history of Fen drainage is especially well documented.[12] John Smeaton, 'founder of civil engineering', was involved in the late eighteenth century. Uncontested success awaited the nineteenth century. The first steam-driven pump was set up in the Fens in 1817, after which more and more powerful pumps were introduced in wetlands across the country, although it should be noted that the first steam engines in the Somerset Levels were found to use more coal than was truly affordable.[13] 'Wind Engines' were established in the Lincolnshire Fens but were thought to be inefficient even before steam was available to replace them. Windmills had not been powerful enough to drain large bodies of water and even the Dutch gave up on the huge Haarlemmermeer, now the site of Schipol airport, until steam was adopted in the mid-nineteenth century. The English, having lagged behind with windmills in the sixteenth- and seventeenth centuries, were by then somewhat ahead, pioneering and improving the steam engines which a government committee from the Netherlands, having viewed them in Cornwall, approved for installation at Haarlemmermeer.

Overall these chronologies suggest most activity in the early seventeenth century, again in a bracket of some decades either side of 1800 and renewed projects during and after the 1850s. The intervening scatter of examples tends to touch very lightly on the mid-eighteenth century, although Sir Joseph Banks's father was involved in the installation of the 'Grand Sluice' above Boston in Lincolnshire in 1764, at the very start of what proved to be a distinct phase of activity during and after the second half of that century. Larger projects reveal a somewhat different and sharper clustering but the mid-eighteenth century stays mainly a gap, raising questions about the attractiveness of agricultural investment at that time or the ability to afford it on a generous scale.

After the major phase of drainage in the early seventeenth century activity quietened down, although it did not quite cease and an expensive, largely failed, attempt to drain Martin Mere, Lancashire, was made by Thomas Fleetwood at the very end of the seventeenth century. As his neighbours had cause to note, expensive it certainly was.[14] Yet in the country at large lesser efforts continued only sporadically until interest was renewed in the 1790s and 1800s. The danger was always that there would be what might be termed rebound flooding, when the newly cut channels began to silt up. Big projects needed a lot of investment, a lot of expertise and the adoption of new technology. The major works of the early seventeenth century had involved fresh expertise—Dutch expertise—and large sums of capital. The recurrence of activity in the years about 1800 drew heavy investment from individual landowners attracted by the prospects or driven by the urgency of high and rising prices for grain and other produce, and who owned enough land and capital to carry out their schemes within the bounds of their estates. Otherwise Acts of parliament were needed to coordinate projects across estate boundaries, since property rights were complex, fiercely defended and tedious to negotiate, which is why under Charles I royal participation had been favoured. Individual enterprises, such as Fleetwood's attempt to drain Martin Mere in the 1690s and minor works in the following century, only slightly muddy the national chronology: an early seventeenth-century phase, a late eighteenth–early nineteenth-century phase, and a nineteenth-century steam phase.

What is curious about this pattern is that the two peaks of large projects in the early seventeenth century and again in the nineteenth century do not fit the standard received chronology of agricultural improvement. They took place either side of the classic eighteenth-century 'agricultural revolution' and not at its height. This was so marked a feature—the first of two great puzzles concerning the history of flooding and drainage—and is so little noticed that it is worth dwelling on the possible reasons; they largely relate to the stimulus of rising prices, the supply of investment capital and the ready availability of expertise. Much of the larger picture of agricultural change, including the introduction of methods from the Low Countries, the subsequent diffusion of fodder crops, and so on, involved comparatively gradual investments by landowners and farmers on their own holdings. Frequent reference is made to the expertise and crops brought back by Royalists returning at the Restoration but it may be supposed that the new rotations and the colonising of the uplands by the plough did not need the enormous capital required by big drainage schemes. Cereal growers within reach of the east coast might benefit from the protection afforded by late seventeenth-century government bounties, but this did not help producers too distant to ship their grain overland to

the ports. In short, for a century after the Restoration the stimulus may have been a little too weak to encourage so-called 'lumpy' investments.

A few Fenland schemes were revived after 1660 but the Dutch were much less in evidence. They did not revive big projects in England after the Restoration, partly because the Dutch Wars were soon to ensue. Why they were not more in evidence agriculturally after the Glorious Revolution remains a puzzle but may be because the Regentiepatriciaat who were on the brink of dominating the United Provinces were inherently passive investors. The absence of London merchants from the mid-eighteenth century scene is a greater surprise but technology had perhaps come close to its limits by that stage and dissuaded every category of investor. Alternatively or additionally there were more enticing outlets for money: canals, turnpikes, enclosures, parks and mansions. Many English landowners were anyhow not necessarily flush with funds. The upheavals of the Civil Wars and Interregnum had left a long shadow, an outstanding example being the 1715 sale of the manor and land at Daylesford, Gloucestershire, by Warren Hastings's grandfather as a result of family 'embarrassments' arising out of the Civil War. Consider too the lament which a widow at Boxwell, Gloucestershire, inscribed on her husband's plaque. He died in 1728, leaving, 'an Estate deeply oppressed with debts incurred by the Adherence of her Husband's Family to the falling Fortunes of the Stuart Kings.'

The role of the Dutch in the big schemes of the first half of the seventeenth century, notably in the Great Level, is always stressed. Understandable though this may be, exaggeration of those episodes is easy in terms of the whole course of drainage in England. Vermuyden's name overshadows everyone else's. The engagement of the Dutch needs to be seen in perspective. For centuries the coasts of the southern North Sea had represented virtually a single economic system, which makes Dutch involvement in England unsurprising and renders priority disputes about the invention of technologies for draining and fishing highly problematic.[15] Early English developments either coincided with or predated the transfers from the Low Countries which are typically credited with them and English backwardness is over-emphasised by the attention paid to immigrants and imported expertise. The possibility of parallel evolution in similar environments is rarely discussed.

Take, for instance, the clyse, a type of big sluice used in the Somerset Levels and designed to prevent the tide pushing flood water back into low-lying areas. The term clyse may be related to the Dutch word for

sluice but the one at Highbridge, Somerset, dated from before 1485 and others were quite early, although they were reinforced between 1770 and 1840 and new ones were added.[16] Or take windmills, which returning crusaders had introduced to England in the twelfth century, but the main adopter phase of which was late by Dutch standards. More generally technical innovation in draining was out of phase in England and the Low Countries and when it came to steam technology the Dutch became the laggards. Wetland reclamation had often predated specific Dutch contributions and there were indigenous English developments. Vermuyden's work in the Fens relied on plans drawn up by John Hunt a generation earlier.

The seventeenth-century Dutch did have a comparative advantage in drainage work. They had engineering expertise derived from their home efforts at reclamation. They had footloose labour willing to move to England, where Vermuyden employed a great number of immigrant hands. The resultant channels and seawalls are visible, whereas softer skills evaporate and are hard to identify; this risks distorting our grasp of which were the more important. The Dutch had evolved the political skills required to negotiate the complex property rights of wetlands, though the biggest schemes needed the support of Charles I to override the resistance of local communities. Dutch firms in the international drainage business have been called the first consulting firms. Above all, they had access to the capital markets of Amsterdam, which were vital for financing projects with long gestation periods and made bringing in the Dutch attractive to Charles I. Vermuyden himself was related to the investor, van Croppenberg.

These endeavours went a long way towards the control of flooding and typically created usable plough-land in place of marshes, bogs, swamps, reed-beds, streams and ponds. They were not always successful at first—a whole medieval abbey had been abandoned on Otmoor in Oxfordshire—but usually they helped to reduce damage by floods. Inundated grassland is poor feed for winter livestock and although it recovers quickly floods can at times be devastating: extreme scenarios do matter. Ironically floods probably did more damage once the land was cultivated and had new farms at risk on it. The effect on land use is well-attested, being obvious to observers, but cost–benefit analysis is hardly possible given the fragmentary sources. It is rarely mentioned in histories of flooding or drainage. What were the relative values of output from the old communal wetland economies and the private enclosed farmland that followed

draining? This is the second of the two great puzzles concerning the history of flooding and drainage, the question being whether there were net gains from drainage or perhaps more realistically how large they were. Several authorities correctly observe that drainage did not mean establishing a productive system where none had existed before but meant replacing virtual hunter-gatherer arrangements by conventional agriculture. It might be possible in a few of the better-documented instances to calculate sample values for the use of the land under regular farming but not for its previous use as commons.

Many publications, especially about the Middle Ages, do refer to the exploitation of natural resources but few probe far enough into ecology to develop even outline pictures of their value.[17] The sources list fishing, wildfowling, egg-collecting, eel-catching, cutting reeds for thatch, turbary (peat-digging) and the recovery of buried timber that could be used for heating and lighting. Boatloads of sedge were sent to the maltsters as fuel. Geese were fed in a large way on the Lincolnshire Fens and goose feathers were plucked elsewhere on a scale supposedly sufficient to furnish the whole country with quills for writing (though really crows' feathers were preferred). Purple moor grass was collected from the tussocks for bedding cattle, which in turn were milked to produce cheese. Some wetlands sent live fish in tubs to the London market. In Lincolnshire Ruff were fattened for the Table [18] On Hampshire's coastal marshes there were salterns producing salt and oysters, while winkles and clams were grown as late as the 1950s. In other places the sea was harnessed to power tide mills. Hemp was grown. Clogs were made from alder. On the Somerset Levels cutting withies for basketmaking was important; before the advent of plastic, baskets were the containers for almost everything. The availability and use of these products differed according to local circumstances and not all were supplied everywhere or all the time. Far from being completely isolated, many wetlands grew enough fodder to agist cattle from elsewhere during the summer and were therefore integrated with the farming of surrounding regions. Wetlands with navigable channels also had links with other regions.

The projectors of drainage schemes found it convenient to condemn the traditional economy of the wetlands in derogatory terms. In an absolute sense, they were wrong because these items had long sustained the communities living there, admittedly too often in a malarial condition. In a relative sense the critics had more of a case, not least because wetlands often overlay excellent soil of which cultivators could make better use. The question, then, is not whether they were wrong but to what extent they exaggerated the defects of traditional systems. Commoners in the Lincolnshire Fens were described as living 'a kind of predatory life' like (it was said) the aborigines of North America did, but were reluctant to change their ways: 'It is no easy task to convince ignorant people that what may appear injurious to themselves, may still be for the benefit of the public at large'—which seems to expect more public spirit from poor people than the improvers themselves exhibited—'with respect to the inclosure of Holland-fen, many who had used every effort to resist it, lived afterwards to see their own folly'.[19] Nevertheless practices in the commoners' traditional economy, rich in natural products, were not completely static because during the nineteenth century wildfowling and use of duck decoys produced birds for the London meat markets. This was on a growing scale, and may reflect improvements in transport and the incentive of increased urban demand for protein. The elasticity of supply of non-agrarian goods could not however match that of farm products since drained land could share in the continual improvement of agricultural methods, whereas in the wetlands opportunities to make technical changes and raise output remained limited.

Changes brought about by drainage projects are typically treated as issues of social justice and have particularly attracted the attention of historians focussed on social and political attitudes. Much notice is taken of violent resistance to enclosure and drainage but unless one believes, as the improvers did, that this delayed drainage for a long time, it does not carry us far with respect to more basic and lasting matters of production or consumption. A detailed count of Parliamentary Acts concerning the Fens approximately accords with other chronologies, reporting only forty-five Acts between 1660 and 1760 but one hundred and seventy four between 1760 and 1800.[20] What this cannot say is how many of the schemes were implemented and the study declares that assessing their economic performance is impossible. Assessment of individual schemes may well be frustrated by a lack of evidence (especially material that might permit comparison with preceding common management) and, even were it possible in certain cases, would undoubtedly be out of reach in the majority of them.

Even so, progress may be made schematically. In terms of the seven standard criteria for evaluating economic systems, the communal systems, over which the Dutch and other entrepreneurs rode roughshod, had not performed well. No economy ever reaches perfection with respect to the criteria, but the deficiency was marked in traditional wetland systems.

They were prone to flooding and hence failed to meet the criterion of resilience to shocks. Nor did they fulfil the criterion of full resource mobilization. As to static allocative efficiency, they may have met this goal within their own confines because wetlands occupied as commons shared resources among their inhabitants. Notwithstanding endless disputes among villages over inter-commoning, whole communities did negotiate collectively, at least in Norfolk. But this did not guarantee maximisation for the larger society or economy. Dynamic allocative efficiency was not met because the communities were conservative and resources were allocated to better use only when reorganised by drainage funded by outsiders. As to dynamic technical efficiency, new methods were not generated internally and crept in from elsewhere to these semi-isolated places slowly, if at all. Static technical efficiency may have been achieved insofar as methods and implements were minutely adjusted to exploiting the wetlands and it is sometimes stated admiringly that their use was well adapted to the environment, in a sort of social parallel of evolution in the Galapagos. No doubt exploitation was regulated by the communities in order to be sustainable—not that lists of the products obtained can tell us how effective this was—and did not overstep the mark in the way a Garrett Hardin might have supposed. Yet adaptation is a conservative goal, capable in principle (if not always in practice) of maintaining the variety of wildlife but at the cost of what in social and economic terms might ironically be called treading water. Potentially the wetlands could be put to more productive use, as finally they were.

In a strict sense, therefore, the old economy of commons in the wetlands, though not nugatory, must have contributed less to the national product than the same land once it was drained. Thirsk, who pioneered the study of wetlands 'before Vermuyden', urged that drainage schemes did not create usable land where there was none but brusquely replaced one system with another: 'the peasants of Axholme had evolved a perfectly satisfactory and profitable farming routine' and she insisted that Vermuyden—in his lifetime—did not prove drained fen was more profitable than when it was un-drained.[21] How long should the experiment be let run, what might be the metric and what the evidence of financial returns? Occasional projectors or farmers might pen their accounts in the evening but commoners did not. 'Before and after' population figures might perhaps be obtained but they would be a remote proxy for profits or living standards. Thirsk adds, nevertheless, the almost contradictory *obiter dictum* that 'ultimately it was necessary and inevitable that the fen should be properly drained'.[22]

The wildlife supported by the marshes is easy to romanticise but the commons remained a drag on growth and hindered their occupants from joining the larger society. Morgan comes to a shrewd conclusion when he points out that, although local communities in the wetlands may have been individually efficient, they could not cope with floodwater from different areas and did not join with other villages to tackle the overall flood problem.[23] They were vulnerable in a way that might have been avoided had they combined with other communities. That would have needed co-operative bodies to enforce and charge for drainage works covering larger areas, bodies that did not merely mark time by ensuring that each township kept up its banks and ditches. The fragmented communal system missed out on economies of scale.

The strength of the commons system lay in satisfying the sole criterion of equality of income, besides almost incidentally going some way towards safeguarding something modern environmentalists would admire—a plethora of wildlife, though insofar as the latter was purposeful it was for the purposes of hunting and fishing.[24] The conservation of wild nature was an externality of un-drained marshes. Nor are assertions about equality of income wholly to be trusted. Reports in the literature of economic development about communities dependent on natural resources do not imply that every family or individual earns the same income. Inter-personal differences in ability, energy, application and taste make that unlikely—note the observation by Jung Chang in *Wild Swans* that even at the height of Maoism in China individuals strove to signal status differences by the tiniest amendments to modes of dress. Nevertheless over the generations in the fenland, an approximate equality of income was perhaps achieved and when things got out of kilter the checks and balances of the communal system probably restored them. On the other hand, marshland did not, and could not, compete with drained farmland as a means, first, of feeding the nation, and secondly of curbing the malaria that was endemic in many wetland districts.

Beyond these undoubted benefits, the broadest consequences of drainage were that they extended the seasons. Consider the county name, Somerset, which is said to allude to the fact that anciently the Levels could be occupied only in summer. This points to the role of drainage in weather-proofing the wetlands. Originally many of them had to be vacated during the winter season even by grazing beasts yet now, up to a point but increasingly, they were reclaimed for year-round use. It is the broadest conclusion of all to say that land drainage was capable of something as fundamental as altering seasonality over wide and potentially rich areas. That exceptional observer in mid-Victorian times, Richard Jefferies, clearly thought drainage possessed that power when he made his fictional professor of agriculture declare that 'if the land had been drained the rain would have done comparatively little damage, and thus they would have been independent of the seasons.' [25] Admittedly drainage brought its own vulnerability, since whereas livestock could be driven elsewhere, crops in the ground are fixed and at risk. The proof of the pudding was that tillage won out in the end.

Ultimately the wetlands represented a sluggish sub-system within the national economy, one which was galvanised chiefly by drainage projects funded and engineered from outside. For present purposes we may leave aside motivation and social consequences, and ignore too the enticing panoramas of wildlife in the swamps in favour of the broader picture. Few naturalists have ever taken F. O. Morris's self-sacrificing view of the draining of Whittlesea Mere in 1851: 'the entomologist… must not repine at even the disappearance of the Large Copper Butterfly, in the face of such vast and magnificent advantages.'[26] Whittlesea was destined for cropping and too much would have been yielded by preserving its traditional uses. Heart and head were at odds. The side effects of diminished natural abundance and the elimination of occasional species were unfortunate prices for bringing the wetlands into the mainstream and making them more productive. Until Victoria's time, it might almost be said, large though receding expanses of marsh had been missing from the country's inventory of cultivated soil. The wetlands had constituted a check on the optimal use of resources.

Notes

1. See for instance John R. L. Allen, 'A Short History of Salt-Marsh Reclamation at Slimbridge Warth and Neighbouring Areas, Gloucestershire', *Transactions of the Bristol and Gloucestershire Archaeological Society* 104 (1986), pp. 139–155.
2. T. H. Baker, *Records of the Seasons, Prices of Agricultural Produce, and Phenomena Observed in the British Isles* (London: Simpkin, Marshall, 1883), p. 139.
3. Michael Williams, *The Draining of the Somerset Levels* (Cambridge: Cambridge University Press, 1970), pp. 87–88; Rose Hewett, 'The Great Flood of 1607', A Forgotten Landscape (website).

4. Nigel Harvey, *The Industrial Archaeology of Farming in England and Wales* (London: Batsford, 1980), p. 23. There is a considerable literature of detailed studies about the history of drainage and floods, mostly dealing with individual wetlands areas. For outstanding accounts see Michael Havinden, *The Somerset Landscape* (London: Hodder and Stoughton, 1981); Jeremy Purseglove, *Taming the Flood* (Oxford: Oxford University Press, 1989); John Virgoe, 'Thomas Fleetwood and the Draining of Martin Mere', *Transactions of the Historic Society of Lancashire and Cheshire* 152 (2003), pp. 27–50; Angus Townley, 'Drainage of the Isle of Axholme', *Crowle Community Forum*, https://crowle.orgwp-contentuploads2015/06; and Elizabeth Griffiths, 'Draining the Coastal Marshes of North-West Norfolk: The Contribution of the Le Stranges at Hunstanton, 1605–1724', *Agricultural History Review* 63 (2) (2015), pp. 221–242. See also the website of the University of Dundee 'Chronology of British Hydrological Events'.
5. Thomas Rudge, *General View of the Agriculture of the County of Gloucestershire* (London: Sherwood, Neely and Jones, 1813), p. 268.
6. H. S. Torrens, 'The Water-Related Work of William Smith (1769–1839)', in J. D. Mather, *200 Years of British Hydrogeology* (Geological Society of London Special Publications, 225, 2004), pp. 15–30.
7. S. B. L. Druce, 'An Account of an Embankment and Cutting in the Parishes of Standlake, Northmoor, Stanton Harcourt, and Eynsham… Made to Protect the District from the Flood Waters of the River Thames', *Journal of the Royal Agricultural Society of England* VI (2nd Series) (1870), pp. 367–374.
8. B. E. Cracknell, *Canvey Island: The History of a Marshland Community* (Leicester: Leicester University Press, 1959), p. 33.
9. Colin Tubbs, *The Ecology, Conservation and History of the Solent* (Chichester: Packard, 1999), p. 57.
10. C. Holmes, 'Drainers and Fenmen: The Problem of Popular Political Consciousness in the Seventeenth Century', in Anthony Fletcher and John Stevenson (eds.), *Order and Disorder in Early Modern England* (London: Cambridge University Press, digital version 2007), pp. 165ff.
11. Griffiths, 'Draining the Coastal Marshes', *Agricultural History Review* (2015).
12. On seventeenth century drainage see e.g. Margaret Albright Knittl, 'The Design for the Initial Drainage of the Great Level of the Fens: An Historical Whodunit in Three Parts', *Agricultural History Review* 55 (1) (2007), pp. 23–50; Padley, *Mid-Lincolnshire* (1882), passim.
13. Havinden, *Somerset Landscape* (1981), pp. 131, 151.

14. 'Captain Fleetwood has had Great Doing at Marton Meer, which notable Exploits have destroyed a World of Powder and made it very dear.' Margaret Blundell, *Blundell's Diary and Letter Book 1702–1728* (Liverpool: Liverpool University Press, 1952), p. 42.
15. Jones, *Revealed Biodiversity* (2014), pp. 116–121.
16. Havinden, *Somerset Landscape* (1981), pp. 135, 149.
17. Purseglove, who had extensive professional field experience, enters most deeply into environmental matters. See Purseglove, *Taming the Flood* (1989).
18. Bird records exist in some numbers for the period after about 1810, when many marshland species were ever more severely hunted, taken in commercial decoys, egged and reduced by reclamation, but specific sources are comparatively rare for earlier times. The eggs collected were presumably above all those of Lapwing and the colonially nesting Black-headed Gull. See Richard Lubbock, *Observations on the Fauna of Norfolk* (Norwich: Jarrold and Sons, 1879), e.g. pp. 96–97, 145; Jones, *Revealed Biodiversity* (2014), pp. 51–52, describes the catching and fattening of Ruff for the table, apparently in the eighteenth- and early nineteenth centuries. This was a more active and long-lasting business in the Netherlands but the similarities in the exploitation of birdlife are clear. Other species are mentioned in England but several had become scarce or extinct early on this side of the North Sea.
19. Padley, *Mid-Lincolnshire* (1882), p. 44.
20. Julian Hoppit, *Britain's Political Economies: Parliament and Economic Life, 1660–1800* (Cambridge: Cambridge University Press, 2017), e.g. pp. 184, 188.
21. Joan Thirsk, *The Rural Economy of England* (London: The Hambledon Press, 1984), p. 162.
22. Thirsk, *Rural Economy* (1984), p. 141.
23. John Emrys Morgan, *Flooding in Early Modern England: Cultures of Coping in Gloucestershire and Lincolnshire* (Ph.D. thesis, Warwick University, 2015). Drainage schemes, too, could spill water to other places and cause floods.
24. Manorial lords were similarly concerned with the amenity of shooting on the marshes. Griffiths, 'Draining the Coastal Marshes', *Agricultural History Review* (2015), p. 234.
25. Richard Jefferies, *Hodge and His Masters* (London: Faber and Faber, 1946), p. 189.
26. Quoted in Jones, *Revealed Biodiversity* (2014), p. xix. Full disclosure: I have been a naturalist all my life but have tried not to let this bias my interpretation of ecological change versus benefits to society.

it out of the question to gather information about the mass of barely reported single house fires. The loss of individual thatched barns was commoner still and even more difficult to count. Currie used a case study of Swavesey, Cambridgeshire, to work back from the stock of houses in 1800 and estimate the average risk of a house being burned down in any one year. This gave him an attrition rate from which to predict the number of houses that should have survived at given dates, the results of the prediction being, as he says himself, 'almost too good to be true'. Only a tiny percentage of surviving dwellings prove to be very old. Currie's conclusion that fire was the chief cause of obligate rebuilding is reassuring and confirms an emphasis on fire history as a cardinal feature of the past.

What history of multi-house fires should we expect? A reduction in the absolute number of fires and their average size after about 1750 was a historically exceptional achievement. It happened despite the fact that populations and settlements were then growing fast. In principle the number and destructiveness of fires 'ought' to have gone on rising in parallel with the growth of towns and villages—*ceteris paribus*, except that everything was not equal. As a general rule measuring fires and settlement sizes is not possible because there is little reliable information about the number or value of buildings by which to assess settlement growth or calculate capital losses directly. In any case the value of loss is not fairly measured by counting buildings destroyed because the number at risk was growing with trade (more goods stored) and industry (a rash of new factories). The increase of warehouse fires in London and other port cities occasioned a swelling loss of capital. In 1861 London's first fire chief, James Braidwood, was killed in a warehouse blaze. Public buildings of note in the capital were also destroyed, which may divert attention from the way fires in groups of dwellings in the country at large were being overcome and the security of the population improved.

In the provinces the best index of risk is population growth. Why should conflagrations not have kept pace with it? When we put the curves of urban population and major fires side by side the results are staggering. Whereas the urban population goes on soaring upwards and the villages start to burst their seams, settlement fires drop away to almost nothing by the middle of the nineteenth century.[5] The difference is the 'fire gap'.[6] In a contiguous group of four southern English counties, there were 47 fires consuming ten or more houses in the period 1650–1699, 32 in 1700–1749, 30 in 1750–1799, and only three in 1800–1849.[7] In most places, reconstruction after these events inserted a ratchet into the

CHAPTER 14

Fires

Upgrading the urban environment by local initiatives and Improvemen Acts helped Victorian town dwellers to forget the muddy streets, wan dering livestock and general air of ***rus in urbe*** that had been familiar t their grandparents. This step-change effectively marked the end of th settlement fires which had been an omnipresent threat and an all-toc often devastating scourge in early modern times. The huge fires passe from memory, the accounts of ghastly destruction written in the ancestr town records went for naught and the English were in denial about t continental-style fire raids of the Civil War.[1] It was left to later antiqu ians to discover the history of fires in their own towns and villages, f of which had escaped altogether and some of which had been levelled the ground more than once.

Stephen Porter, Michael Turner and I assembled a gazetteer of 5 urban fire disasters from local histories, briefs soliciting alms for the s ferers, and miscellaneous sources.[2] Unpublished research has expan the total without much altering the time distribution. In what follows concentration is on south-central and south-west England, the figures which are representative of Lowland England although some periph counties were scarcely affected.[3] The national data can be used to th light on a variety of questions and C. R. J. Currie drew on them to culate the time pattern of surviving houses.[4] He rightly pointed out the cumulative effect of fires affecting only one, two or three houses have been as significant as the impact of the intermittent 'big' ones, w we defined as destroying at least 10 houses at a time, because we fc

E. L. Jones, *Barriers to Growth*, Palgrave Studies in Economic History,
https://doi.org/10.1007/978-3-030-44274-3_14

cycle of fire. This is an important point. Where once there had been a high chance that a big fire would recur within a generation or so, the eighteenth-century switch from mud walls, external timbering and straw-covered roofs to brick-and-tile went a long way towards interrupting the cycle. There were occasions when a fire driven by particularly strong, dry winds overpowered the new materials and all struggles to quench it failed, but normally the better defences prevailed.

Improved construction was the main cause. Firefighting technology played only a supporting role. The manual fire pumps and hoses that originated from Holland and were sold into rural England by London makers were puny relative to a really good blaze, although when they could be got to a fire in time (some were small enough to be carried into a house and up the stairs) they may possibly have been worth their weight in gold. Neighbouring places appear to have acquired them at dates that were not far apart, presumably imitating one another and succumbing to the fashion for buying them. There were places in Dorset and Devon where old wooden models were employed as late as the 1940s, by which time lighter and superior metal versions were available. Yet although it is not known how many fires were ever nipped in the bud by them, manual fire engines of any design simply could not halt the worst blazes and were not the chief means of suppressing the scourge of fire.[8] Chains of men handing buckets of water to one another might sometimes win, too, although again not when tackling the worst fires whatever system they adopted for organising the chain.[9] Part of the duty of the civic or parish authorities was to make sure everyone kept a bucket to hand. 'We present Mr. Miles, ye dancing master, for having no fire bucket', say the borough archives of eighteenth-century Marlborough, amidst a recitation of similar offences so tedious and unending as to show that people either had short memories or tried to free-ride on the precautions taken by their more prudent neighbours. Backsliders might be fined but no more drastic measures were taken against them.

Many villages and even towns were tinderboxes. Originally dwellings were thatched, a practice that lasted a long time and in a measure persists today, although modern cottage roofs are usually better tended than our ancestors could afford. Popular books of old photographs establish the point. Barns were thatched and together with hayricks were crowded next to farmhouses in the centre of many a village and small town. A simple method, effective against the spread of fire in such places if it could be brought into play fast enough, was to pull off the roof thatch before it could combust. Parishes kept communal hooks for the purpose. Not only might adjacent properties be spared but burning or smouldering thatch could be stopped from falling into the building and destroying the contents.

A number of fires devastated whole villages while the inhabitants were out in the harvest fields and before they could get back home. The harvest season tended to be dry. Crawley, Hampshire, was almost obliterated like this in 1738. At other times there were odd twists of fortune. In July, 1832, at Bradninch, Devon, when sparks from the dry furze at a bakehouse were blown onto thatched roofs, the 'Old King William', being tiled, did not catch fire and stayed the flames in one direction. The good luck was that a thatcher, coming home from work, straightaway stripped the thatch from the roof of one house and stopped the fire in the next.[10] The bad luck was that for all his efforts the fire turned into a blaze destroying forty-eight other houses, the guildhall, the gaol and the Baptist chapel. Bradninch was unsurprisingly described by its monographer as 'this inflammable little place'.[11]

English settlements were crowded, their property rights were intermingled, and no authorities regularly overrode individual rights. Groups of inhabitants seldom agreed well enough to rearrange ground plans. When they did, they may not have acted in the public interest—after another fire at Bradninch in the winter of 1835–1836, the owners of several plots, working in concert, moved the pegs before rebuilding could begin so that each of them could usurp a section of roadway.[12] Despite protests they got away with it. Ironically their forebears had set a better example by altering the town plan after a fire in the winter of 1683–1684. Both sides of a whole street were then cleared so that it was straightened and became New Street. Yet although the opportunity is said to have been taken to widen or straighten roads in a number of other towns, civic activism on any scale was unusual.

Crowding, and a preference for locating one's workshop on the busy street, meant that another practice which might really have helped to reduce the incidence of fire was rarely chosen. This was building away from the neighbours and introducing a firebreak of sheer distance. There was usually too little land to spare from farming in England to do this. In nucleated towns and villages the only routinely available firebreaks were churchyards and market squares. Coupled with the fact that churches were usually built of stone, churchyards preserved them from many a fire sweeping through the streets around and occasionally blocked its spread altogether. On the other hand, market places commonly succumbed to private encroachments in early times, increasing the density of settlement and the risk.

The danger from yards and workshops which stored timber and other flammable materials and used naked flames for everyday tasks is remarked in the records of hundreds of towns and villages. Farms were often on the village streets, with barns and outbuildings crammed with hay and other agricultural produce standing right next to them. All this raised the level of risk. In the market towns reroofing in non-flammable materials, initially with tile, increasingly with Welsh slate brought in by canal, was carried out earlier than in the villages. Townspeople could better afford to upgrade their properties than villagers and urban upgrading was sometimes enforced by special enactments and local by-laws which were beyond the power of village elders. Moreover, town dwellers could be required to replace flammable materials on their houses with less of the contentiousness that would have been associated with altering street plans. In the course of things, new houses might be built in fashionable materials, which happened incrementally. But it seemed to require the shock of a fire to induce all owners to replace and insure their dwellings at the same time. The poor, understandably, could not afford insurance and stood to lose everything. They tended to be forced into rented housing in back streets. When fires recurred they reinforced the rising inequality of wealth and income that accompanied eighteenth-century growth. More than anyone, the poor relied on communal efforts to keep fire at bay.

Major fires ceased a little earlier in towns than villages. The spread of fires was commonly frustrated once some owners had replaced thatch with tile. Consider the period from the eighteenth century to the mid-nineteenth century: among fires between 1700 and 1749, 48 per cent occurred in villages but only 35 per cent in towns, whereas between 1750 and 1799 33 per cent were village fires but only 15 per cent were town fires.[13] The absolute number of fires was falling in all classes of settlement but progress came first in the towns. The value of even partial reroofing was demonstrated at Dorchester, Dorset, where a fire in 1775, 'raged with great fury for several hours, taking very irregular directions, making great havock amongst the thatched houses, and passing those which were roofed with tiles or slates'.[14] Likewise at Beaminster, Dorset, poor quality houses were destroyed in a fire of 1781 but stone houses, erected after an earlier fire in 1684 by all who could then afford to do so, escaped.[15] There was a Matthew effect: 'for whosoever hath, to him shall more be given...'. For a long time tiles were beyond the purses of many, but since even partly tiled settlements were safer than those that were all of thatch, free riding on the neighbours could be a successful gambit.

Contemporaries were well aware of the advantages conferred by tile roofs. As early as 1624 nineteen inhabitants of the village of Wylye certified to the Wiltshire Quarter Sessions that they, 'do think Willyam Lock and his wife persons very fit to keep an ale house or house of entertainment in this our parish of Weyley and the rather because their ho. is tylled and without danger of fire'.[16] Already that year the parishioners had demanded that a brewer and baker be stopped from using a fire without erecting a chimney, flue or stone wall at least four feet above it. He had almost set the 'town' (the village) alight once or twice, his '*being a thatched house*', as they emphasised. Admittedly reroofing was not absolute proof against the severest fires, for example an eyewitness reported of the great conflagration that destroyed Blandford, Dorset, in 1731, 'the Thatch'd buildings soon consumed; the stronger parts of the Town remained till towards night'.[17] Yet there were so many places where non-flammable roofing did halt a fire front that tiling or slating was recognised as the best single precaution. Buildings were transformed into durable structures different from the fragile ones vulnerable to wrecking by fire in earlier times.

A century or more was needed for the market towns as a whole to emerge clad in non-flammable materials and for local authorities to succeed in having the hazardous trades of distilling, candle making, soap boiling, tanning, baking and brewing moved out to the fringes of the built-up area. The fringes were of course not far away. Until the second half of the seventeenth century and often later, towns would have seemed to modern eyes like quaint villages. Except on the stone belts, where settlement fires were uncommon, buildings were constructions of timber frames filled in with wattle hurdles plastered with mud. The mud was dried, hardened and lime-washed, and there was a tendency for whole towns to sport the same colour. The original roofs were of the offending thatch. Many of the houses were huddled along twisting streets and invariably close behind them lay clutters of outhouses, sheds, barns and workshops. Capital diverted to replanning and rehousing could not be used to re-start businesses. Even though converting houses to non-flammable materials would have guarded against future losses, artisans either did not have ready money or were inclined to delay and put the risk out of their minds. After all, what in retrospect appear to have been terrifyingly frequent fires might have seemed to men making year-to-year investment decisions as something likely to strike only at long intervals. Their grandparents or parents may have been hit whereas they thought they could discount the threat.

Both the canalising of rivers after the Restoration and the canal age about a century later reduced the price of coal, which was needed to bake brick and tile. The frontier of brick houses then moved spatially westwards from London and the southeast and sociologically downwards from rich to poor. London and its fashions had always exerted a formative influence over the remainder of the south. Anthony Wood said that the burghers of Oxford registered the example of London after a fire they suffered in 1190 and rebuilt in stone and slate, not wood and straw (i.e. thatch).[18] Even the Oxford poor then erected high walls of stone between every four or six houses but this precaution was not always repeated or copied elsewhere. Across the country fire remained an ever-present danger, which was well known without always prompting desirable counter-measures. Underestimating the risk of fire is a perpetual failing, current consumption tending to trump long-term security. Householders in the Middle Ages and in some places much later were required to cover or douse their hearths when the curfew bell rang at the end of the day. They were obliged to keep a couvre-feu for the purpose—a once-ubiquitous item of material culture that has vanished as silently as the stage waggon. A big change in the security of towns, and their appearance, was a long time coming, not until the stipulations of the London Fire Acts were widely copied at the start of the eighteenth century.

Other towns were dwarfed by London, which drew produce from further and further west, and radiated out its vast influence in return. In the 1670s the Hampshire agriculturist, John Worlidge, was so impressed he declared that if the best London practice in building were spread, 'our *England* in a few Ages... would represent to the view of all, what *Middlesex* it's *Epitome* now doth'.[19] In important measure Worlidge's prophecy came true. If the remainder of the country did not become fully brick-built like Holland at least it became like Middlesex. The boxy, flat-fronted style of brick house insisted on by the London Building Acts of Queen Anne's reign, as less risky than exterior timbering and overhanging stories, was imitated elsewhere. Builders' pattern books spread the style to all who could afford it.

The post-Great Fire rebuilding of London was therefore said in 1801 to have produced a hitherto unknown but subsequently unceasing spirit of improvement.[20] Smaller towns began in the eighteenth century to afford to copy London styles because of the expansion of their own trade. They were rich enough to draw skilled craftsmen back from the metropolis to the provinces, as newspaper advertisements confirm, or it might be back from the London which had drawn them away like a magnet after the Great Fire.[21] Moreover there were smallish towns in England which rediffused the novelties. Villages, which were all satellites of some market town, picked up the ideas in turn. City fashions eventually trickled right down. Many villages have a few very urban-looking houses that belonged to professional gentlemen or were genteel retirement homes at surprisingly early dates.

The urban landscape was markedly transformed in central streets, especially in the larger or more prosperous places. This might have happened anyhow through the upgrading of private houses, but piecemeal initiatives did not satisfy the desire to improve or prettify public spaces. That needed effective local government. The saving grace was the Improvement Trust.[22] New bodies of Improvement Commissioners were formed to oversee paving, road building and road and path mending, lighting, watching (including fire watching), scavenging and supplying fresh water. Whereas only four new sets of Commissioners had been established during the entire second quarter of the eighteenth century, more and more were founded in each following decade, up to the astonishing total of 160 in the 1790s alone.

These men—inevitably men—could levy special rates to fund their schemes. Where informal negotiation had proved inadequate, the Improvement Acts were strong enough to force through change, of which a visible sign was the widening of streets, although they were seldom rerouted. The colonisation of sidewalks by shops and their clutter, as well as the intrusion of whole buildings into market places, was now frowned on. This gave rise, where need be, to the compulsory purchase and demolition of intruding houses. Perhaps it was helpful that the Commissioners worked in ordinary times rather than during the stress and confusion that followed fires, when haste militated against vision. Against this, truly drastic alterations of town or village plans were unusual. Places without Improvement Acts or powers like those which the London Fire Court acquired after the Great Fire were at a disadvantage and remained medieval in aspect the longest. Quite apart from the difficulty of securing agreement in places without firm by-laws, people who had suffered from conflagrations were eager to get back in business and likely to feel that following the old building lines would be quicker than negotiating changes. Even in London there were people who were disappointed because original property bounds were so often retained: Mathew Hale had been no Parisian Haussmann after all.

Just occasionally we can find a commentary on the cumulative improvement of a given place, for instance in 1784 an inhabitant of Chichester, Sussex, made a note in his old age of every tiny advance: a replacement conduit, a wooden fish shambles renewed in stone, the footpaths paved and fenced, a new assembly room built, a new and wider bridge built, and the old town gate removed.[23] 'I have seen', reported the old man, 'almost the whole city and town new built or new faced, a spirit of emulation in this way having run through the whole'. The inhabitants of most of the larger towns in southern England might have said the same, the spirit of emulation seeping down to smaller and smaller places.

The human habitat was being refashioned. Boxy brick houses were easier to clean and keep free of rats, while their big sash windows let in more light. Outdoors, the streets were more orderly, easier to clean too, and easier (though never actually easy) to keep free from straying animals. The London authorities had first recognised that building in brick was valuable for reducing dirt-induced diseases and others soon noted the same. Better public health through crude measures by obscure town officials was therefore responsible for part of the eighteenth-century growth of population. This was probably checked, however, when increasing numbers of the poor swamped the housing available to them and to some extent frustrated the improvements of the age.

In Georgian times, town centres became almost genteel and the middle classes could live lives of quiet enjoyment when many a small place held dances in the assembly rooms, and hosted card games and floral feasts in the inns. Improvements and better building joined other developments in cutting the risk of fire. The picture was mixed because not everyone's dwellings shared this mannered graciousness. In back alleys, crowded courts and subdivided houses the life of the poor became more and more crowded and not as sanitary as the authorities would have liked. Nevertheless, the conclusion must be that the suppression of settlement fires had removed an economic impediment and permitted a flowering of middle-class and civic building.

Notes

1. See however Stephen Porter, 'The Fire-Raid in the English Civil War', *War and Society* 2 (1984), pp. 27–40.
2. E. L. Jones, S. Porter, and M. Turner, *A Gazetteer of English Urban Fire Disasters, 1500–1900* (Norwich: Historical Geography Research Series 13, 1984).
3. Site inspections and the help of local historians confirm for instance that Herefordshire was little troubled by settlement fires. In most counties the more searches are carried out, the more fires are found, although the details are often sparse.
4. C. R. J. Currie, 'Time and Chance: Modelling the Attrition of Old Houses', *Vernacular Architecture* 19 (1988), pp. 1–9.
5. See for parallels E. L. Jones and L. E. Frost, 'The Fire Gap and the Greater Durability of Nineteenth-Century Cities', *Planning Perspectives* 4 (1989), pp. 333–347.
6. Critics of this approach have offered no viable alternative and seem resistant to any form of conceptualisation.
7. E. L. Jones, 'The Reduction of Fire Damage in Southern England, 1650–1850', *Post-Mediaeval Archaeology* II (1968), p. 142. The counties are Berkshire, Dorset, Hampshire and Wiltshire.
8. Some manual pumps have been disposed of by obtuse municipalities but a very large number survive and attract hobbyist interest. Accounts are typically uncritical but a most comprehensive article by Richard Bull demonstrates their deficiencies: 'The Fire Engine and Lyme's Great Fires', Lyme Regis Museum, *Paper no. 10*, 2013.
9. On this and other practical aspects of fire-fighting and the vulnerability of settlements I am grateful to Julia Hunt, 'Living with Fire', Aldbourne Community Heritage Group, 23 Sept 2019.
10. Charles Crosleigh, *Bradninch* (London: Alexander Moring, 1911), p. 108.
11. Crosleigh, *Bradninch* (1911), p. 113.
12. Crosleigh, *Bradninch* (1911), p. 110.
13. Jones, 'Reduction of Fire Damage' (1968), p. 148.
14. John Hutchins, *The History and Antiquities of the County of Dorset* (Westminster, 1861, 3rd edition), p. 341.
15. Richard Hine, *The History of Beaminster* (Taunton, 1914), pp. 123, 128.
16. B. Howard Cunningham, *Records of the County of Wilts* (Devizes, 1932), p. 77.
17. Quoted by D. Gardiner, *Companion into Dorset* (London: Methuen, 1949, 4th edition), p. 236.
18. Ruth Fasnacht, *A History of the City of Oxford* (Oxford: Basil Blackwell, 1954), p. 28.
19. J. W. Gent [John Worlidge], *Systema Agriculturae* (London: J.C. for T. Dring, 1675), p. 230.

20. William Heberden, Jun., quoted by B. Benjamin, Introduction, *Population and Disease in Early Industrial England* (Gregg International Publishers, 1973), p. 77.
21. G. A. Cranfield, *The Development of the Provincial Newspaper* (Oxford: Clarendon Press, 1962), p. 212.
22. See E. L. Jones and M. E. Falkus, 'Urban Improvement and the English Economy in the Seventeenth and Eighteenth Centuries', *Research in Economic History* 4 (1979), pp. 193–233.
23. Steer (ed.), Francis W. Steer, *The Memoirs of James Spershott* (Chichester: City Council, 1962), pp. 18ff.

Conclusion

Among the themes running quietly through long-term English economic history are the slow reforming of institutions, better allocation of resources, improved techniques and materials, and greater resilience to shocks. Onto a scene becoming by historical standards more flexible and secure, eventually sprang the great disruptive technologies of cotton-producing machinery, steam power and the railway. Neither the country nor the world was ever the same again. This book is not concerned with that well-rehearsed story but with the background developments whereby, despite the inertia, corruption and rent-seeking of early times, the economy became successively more responsive to market signals. It argues that the removal of barriers to better allocation and more safety was an integral part of the growth process.

The book's aim is not to suggest a unique English triumphalism, merely to chart the prelude to the rapid changes of the decades about 1800. It suggests that histories which concentrate on the earth-shattering arrival of industrialisation are incomplete. Seen against the turning of the centuries the change arrived suddenly enough but it did not appear out of the blue. Precursors of almost every technological novelty may be found, yet it is not the inventions that surprise as much as the rapidity of uptake. Even more noteworthy was the waning of resistance. Society in a corrupt, rent-seeking country had become sufficiently open barely to notice the shift in economic gravity towards Manchester and the north, and fluid enough to cash in on their eventual swift ascent.

E. L. Jones, *Barriers to Growth*, Palgrave Studies in Economic History,
https://doi.org/10.1007/978-3-030-44274-3

Pre-industrial relocation is perceived by scholars as the rise or fall of little places and not presented as a whole in the way it deserves. England was defined by its absorptive features and this was what eased the path to change. The creaking, jarring and groaning of the developing society and economy were in a minor key compared with the turn-round when industrialisation arrived in continental countries. The English economy was able to make fruitful use of new methods and new devices first, and no political upheaval was needed before they were accepted. De Tocqueville claimed that at the end of the eighteenth century the French were far in advance of other people in their move towards democracy. His interpretation may be uncongenial to the English but his survey of the hollowing out of archaic and aristocratic institutions in France reveals an underlying transformation belied by appearances.[1] This goes a long way towards explaining how France was able to industrialise relatively fast in England's wake; it was not simply the ability to borrow or replicate English technology that mattered but the organisational arrangements which let it be introduced. The French Revolution's abolition of privileges and exclusive rights had removed 'the institutions of the Middle Ages and... the obstacles to progress'. Furthermore, Napoleon's imposition of administrative modernity elsewhere in Western Europe enhanced a responsiveness that England had already muddled its way towards. Had that part of the continent remained sunk in medievalism it could not have followed the industrial path in a mere couple of generations. Admittedly, Napoleon had centuries of social and business development and interconnection across Western Europe to build on.[2] Industrialisation required more forceful state intervention in Eastern Europe.[3]

In England especially prolonged change had opened the way. Themes that come through are the decline of deadweight costs, such as the reduction of expenditure on defensive and ecclesiastical buildings; a shift of assets to people supposedly more likely to exploit them (for all the caveats the Dissolution must come to mind); the avoidance of renewed conflict after the Civil War; and the exploitation of underused resources of many types. Impediments to growth only gradually wasted away over the centuries but waste away many of the truly vexatious did. An exception was property law to which, despite the semblance of legality, access was in practice severely restricted by its cost. Conceivably the distributional consequences were more harmful than any actual hampering of resource use; most people may have been excluded from the courts but those with property, including entrepreneurs, could deploy the law to their own advantage.

Given the inequalities of wealth, income and status, the avoidance of renewed civil violence over the centuries after the Restoration is at first sight puzzling. It was partly because Puritan opposition moved grudgingly away from politics, deliquescing into a religious nonconformity that sank into sects and never again presented a united front. Cromwell's officers were reincorporated into the conservative society from which they had come. Search as they may, historians of the working class find vastly more cases of oppression than concerted resistance to exploitation. Few disturbances transpired except riots about enclosure in occasional parishes and the uprising of foolishly trusting farm workers called the Last Labourers' Revolt. The leading Cromwellians, including Oliver himself, had long since repudiated Leveller demands for manhood suffrage.[4] They were 'gentlemen' and their struggle had not been aimed at restructuring property, only at guaranteeing it for their own faction. After the Restoration, conservative landowners and merchants (who often bought estates) were happy to restore, entrench and intensify a class-based rural society which limited social mobility and enterprise.

De Tocqueville said of France that all exclusive rights had been destroyed leaving only one, that of property.[5] The future struggle, he proclaimed, would be between those who owned property and those who did not: 'the great battlefield will be property…' England also witnessed the survival of old rights to property which established it as an arena of inequality. It took much urbanisation and industrialisation before the propertyless ever mobilised in effective trade unions. They had been virtually, sometimes literally, disarmed. Rural labour had been excluded from politics. Unsurprisingly, therefore, freedom, decent education and scientific curiosity remained the prerogative of small circles and did not draw on society's potential talent; it need hardly be said that the talent of the mass of womenfolk was ignored. These self-inflicted wounds were not recognised as such.

Participants in economic activity nevertheless remained numerous. Enterprises were small and there were far more small farms in 1660 than later. Business operators, including farmers, were not merely involved in their private managerial decisions but many were parties to communal agreements about resource allocation. If there is one thread that appears and reappears in sphere after sphere and century after century it was the difficulty of negotiating change in communal systems, where mindsets did

Personal temperaments and non-economic motives create a *pointilliste* impression, which means that short-period studies of single firms and industries, single estates, single parishes, or even single counties may mislead. This has the makings of a split between those approaching economic history in terms of national aggregates or averages and those interested in local individuality. Economists and like-minded economic historians concentrate on the big new movements. They are lumpers who label phenomena according to the a priori categories of economic theory and are content with highly generalised databases. Historians, especially local historians, are splitters who take the view that a single exception can invalidate a theory and scour the sources for an unfamiliar angle from which to describe the past—description being the order of their day. It is probable that both sides will miss something, the former transcending or traducing reality and the latter too shy of seeking unifying features beneath the evidential load.

Concentrating on the decay of obstacles to growth appears likely to place the emphasis on the historian's side, on grounded reality and on recounting myriad manoeuvrings of individuals. This is not the aim, which is more analytical, trying to find unity among the successive, long-term, seemingly unconnected advances that dismantled barriers. Procedures that may have created resistance to innovation and the ways in which resistance was overcome are extracted from the welter of contradictory impulses. Contradictory indeed: both institutional and physical advances meant to succour development could choke it. They could have unintended consequences. Planting new crops and agisting cattle for growing markets aroused conflict with tithe owners, which was just one example where supporters of established institutions became more intransigent in the face of change. Property bounds were fiercely defended and opportunities to replan settlements after fires were missed. Digging ditches might bring rebound flooding if they were not well designed or deep enough to prevent silt piling up. Marginally better roads and bridges could not always handle the traffic that went on increasing after 1750. Growth could not be anticipated with enough certainty to elicit the 'lumpy' investments needed to cope with every difficulty. It may be speculated that economic expansion came as close as it ever did to stalling in the 1770s, when canals, turnpikes and enclosures all competed for scarce capital. Interest rates rose after 1770 and especially between 1776 and 1783, while much Dutch capital was repatriated in 1777. Only the capital markets of the end of the eighteenth century and during the nineteenth century were liquid enough to make room for the future. Arguing for 'delayed onset industrialisation' would overstep the mark but there may have been a hiccough.

What can account for the success of productive changes in the face of the inertia of special interests? Taking the outcomes for granted—at one moment adopting innovation, at the next clinging to grandfather's ways—explains nothing. Nor does extolling the progress that was made tell us why the market-minded were able to prevail. Citing self-interest will not do: those who resisted novelties evidently thought their own self-interest was better served by not rocking the boat. The few theo ries available to account for this tension are exceedingly general. We may discount Hardin's vision of peasants destroying their own resource base by overstocking the commons. That was usually reined in by their neighbours in conclave. We might perhaps appeal to the aggressive egos who secured privileges or large shares for themselves (the right to separate grazing rights from properties, say, and sell them on) or who persuaded their fellows to adopt some new routine or new crop. But that would make history a lottery which depended on 'human nature', imprecise and analytically unhelpful.

We are left with C. R. Hallpike and C. E. Ayres. Both offer very broad interpretations. Hallpike's swipe at the use of evolutionary logic to explain change in tribal societies rests on the fact that these small communities were not situated within overarching markets. A lack of competition, an effect of poor communications, meant that almost random items from the natural world were venerated, always different ones from those worshipped by the neighbours. In this way Hallpike accounts for the bewildering variety of sacred objects found in the less-developed world. Pre-industrial England partly differed. It did not lack all overarching institutions, because it had the church and some organs of state, but there was sufficient isolation—sufficiently restricted information markets—to mean that solutions to domestic or husbandry problems were diverse. The most efficient means took time to prevail. England was a half-way house that was not immune to all outside influence but mainly adopted best practice when expanding markets fostered competition.

Ayres's approach introduces more of a mechanism for change. To his mind, conservative institutions offered defences against disruptive technologies and observable history was the result of the tension between them. Conflict and sluggish adoptions were to be expected since existing interests were resistant to change. This does offer a framework consistent with the impediments we have described, all the disputes about change

Index

E. L. Jones, *Barriers to Growth*, Palgrave Studies in Economic History, https://doi.org/10.1007/978-3-030-44274-3

The manufacturer's authorised representative in the EU is Springer Nature Customer Service Centre GmbH, Europaplatz 3, 69115 Heidelberg, Germany. If you have any concerns regarding our products, please contact ProductSafety@springernature.com

Printed and bound by CPI Group (UK) Ltd, Croydon, CR0 4YY
28/09/2026
02224083-0009